The Trap

Polish Theatre Archive

A series of books edited by Daniel Gerould, Graduate School, City University of New York, USA

Volume 1
To Steal a March on God
Hanna Krall
translated and with an introduction by Jadwiga Kosicka

Volume 2
Alternative Theatre in Poland
1954–1989
Kathleen Cioffi

Volume 3
Country House
Stanisław Ignacy Witkiewicz
translated and with an introduction by Daniel Gerould

Volume 4
The Trap
Tadeusz Różewicz
translated by Adam Czerniawski
and with an introduction by Daniel Gerould

Volume 5
Polish Romantic Drama
Three plays in English translation
selected, edited and with an introduction by Harold B. Segel

Additional volumes in preparation:

The Mannequins' Ball
Bruno Jasieński
translated and with an introduction by Daniel Gerould

Encounters with Tadeusz Kantor
Krzysztof Miklaszewski

This book is part of a series. The publisher will accept continuation orders which may be cancelled at any time and which provide for automatic billing and shipping of each title in the series upon publication. Please write for details.

The Trap

by Tadeusz Różewicz

authorized translation by
Adam Czerniawski

with an introduction by
Daniel Gerould

harwood academic publishers
Australia • Canada • China • France • Germany • India
Japan • Luxembourg • Malaysia • The Netherlands • Russia
Singapore • Switzerland • Thailand • United Kingdom

Copyright © 1997 OPA (Overseas Publishers Association) Amsterdam B.V.
Published in The Netherlands by Harwood Academic Publishers.

All rights reserved.

No part of this book may be reproduced or utilized in any form or by any means, electronic or mechanical, including photocopying and recording, or by any information storage or retrieval system, without permission in writing from the publisher.

Amsteldijk 166
1st Floor
1079 LH Amsterdam
The Netherlands

All enquiries concerning performing rights should be directed to Adam Czerniawski, Hawthornden Castle, Lasswade, EH18 1EG, Scotland.

British Library Cataloguing in Publication Data

Różewicz, Tadeusz
   The Trap. – (Polish Theatre Archive; v. 4)
   1. Polish drama – 20th century – Translations into English
   I. Title
   891.8'5'2'7

ISBN 3-7186-5856-9 (paperback)

The cover illustration shows, from the left, Jolanta Zalewska (Felice), Edwin Petrykat (Father) and Olgierd Łukazewicz (Franz) in the 1992 Wrocław production of *The Trap*. Photo: Stefan Okołowicz.

CONTENTS

Introduction to the Series	vii
List of Plates	ix
Chronology of the Life of Tadeusz Różewicz	xi
Introduction: The Open Theatre of Tadeusz Różewicz	xiii
Prologue	1
The Trap	9
Selective Bibliography	95

INTRODUCTION TO THE SERIES

The *Polish Theatre Archive* makes available in English translation major works of Poland's dramatic literature as well as monographs and critical studies on Polish playwrights, theatre artists and stage history. Although emphasis is placed on the contemporary period, the *Polish Theatre Archive* also encompasses the nineteenth-century roots of modern theatre practice in Romanticism and Symbolism. The individual plays will contain authoritative introductions that place the works in their historical and theatrical contexts.

DANIEL GEROULD

LIST OF PLATES

1. Tadeusz Różewicz.   x

2. World première of *The Trap* at Den Nationale Scene, Bergen, Norway, 15 October 1983.   86

3–5. Scenes from the 1984 production of *The Trap*, Theatre Studio, Warsaw.   87–89

6. *The Trap*, Teatr Wybrzeże, Gdańsk, 1984.   90

7. *The Trap*, Maxim Gorki Theater, East Berlin, 1985.   91

8. *The Trap*, Serbian National Theatre, Novi Sad, Yugoslavia, 1988.   92

9. Wiener Festwochen and Teatr Studio co-production of *The Trap* at the Wiener Festwochen, 1991.   93

10. *The Trap*, Teatr Polski, Wrocław, 1992.   94

1. Tadeusz Różewicz. Photo: Adam Hawałej.

CHRONOLOGY OF THE LIFE OF TADEUSZ RÓŻEWICZ

1921	Born October 9, in Radomsko, where his father is a petty official.
1937–8	Edits a school magazine in which his first poems appear.
1939–42	During German occupation works as a messenger, clerk, and carpenter's apprentice.
1942	Joins the Resistance and attends secret military classes.
1943–4	Active as a soldier in a partisan unit where he edits an underground magazine and publishes prose and poetry. Elder brother Janusz, an Intelligence officer in the Resistance, executed by the Gestapo.
1945	Completes his secondary education in Częstochowa and studies art history at the Jagellonian University in Kraków.
1947	With the publication of *Anxiety*, his first collection of poetry, wins recognition as a major new poet.
1949	Marries his fiancée, a fellow-member of the Resistance. Visits Prague and develops a life-long interest in Kafka.
1950	Moves to Gliwice where his first son is born. Visits Hungary. Writes his first play, *Out of Hiding* (unpublished and unperformed). Starts to publish many volumes of poems and stories.
1957	Visits Paris. Second trip to Prague.
1960	Begins career as a dramatist with *The Card Index*, published and performed in a severely censored version.
1962–8	Writes many widely-performed plays: *The Laocoon Group, The Witnesses, Gone out, The Funny Old Man, The Interrupted Act, The Old Woman Broods*.
1968	Moves to Wrocław. Writes *Birth Rate*.
1973	Writes *Mariage Blanc*.
1975	First trip to the US. Writes *The Hunger Artist*.
1976	*Marriage Blanc* is publicly condemned as "smut" by Cardinal Wyszyński.
1981	Completes *The Trap* in November. World première at the Dramatic Theatre, Warsaw, is cancelled because of Martial Law and the closing of the theatre.
1982	*The Trap* is published in theatre journal *Dialog* as well as in book form.
1983	October 15 world première of *The Trap* in Bergen, Norway. Directed by Krystyna Skuszanka with sets and costumes by Krzysztof Pankiewicz.

CHRONOLOGY

1984	January 7 Polish première of *The Trap* in Wrocław at the Współczesny Theatre, directed by Kazimierz Braun. January 15 première in Warsaw at the Studio Theatre directed by Jerzy Grzegorzewski.
1990	Television version (Warsaw) of *The Trap* directed by the filmmaker, Stanisław Różewicz, the playwright's brother.
1991	"Interrupted conversation"—a prologue to *The Trap* is published in *Dialog*.
1992	Première of *The Trap* at the Teatr Polski in Wrocław directed by Jerzy Jarocki.

INTRODUCTION

The Open Theatre of Tadeusz Różewicz

Although he has not written anything new for the theatre since *The Trap* (*Pułapka*, 1981), Tadeusz Różewicz remains the most provocative and original Polish playwright of the post-war period. His probing of the boundaries traditionally assigned to theatre has put him in the forefront of artistic innovators along with Kantor and Grotowski. Outstanding directors have sought to realize his work in production, despite inherent tensions between the author's radically experimental propositions and the nature of theatre itself.

With his first performed play, *The Card Index* (*Kartoteka*, 1960), Różewicz (already a major poet) introduced a new theatrical language of fragmented structure and imagistic montage, which, at first, seemed disorienting but eventually came to be accepted as a quintessential expression of post-war sensibility. For the generation of Poles who came of age in 1939, the experience of wholesale death and destruction during the war and occupation had rendered obsolete notions of beauty, high ideals, and noble words. A new aesthetic, Różewicz felt, had to take Auschwitz as its basic premise. Literature as it had existed until then was simply a lie. Repudiating ideologies, moral judgements and intellectual speculations as empty abstractions, the author of *The Trap* clung to the bare facts of human life as the only truths and the only values.

Of Polish playwrights since 1945, Różewicz has been the most restless experimenter with form. In a number of his works for the stage he undertakes an ontological analysis of theatre that questions the very assumptions that make performance possible. Recognizing that reality will not submit to the artistic conceptions of the past, the Polish poet strives to go beyond the limits of the genre. In rejecting hierarchical notions of high and low, foreground and background, beginning, middle and end, Różewicz essays a kind of drama that starts at point zero with an undifferentiated aleatory mass of sights and sounds and persists as pure duration.

Różewicz has repeatedly voiced the "desire to write a play that would be both truly realistic and at the same time poetic." By rendering poetry realistic and realism poetic, the playwright has achieved his goal in many of his dramas. His work is realistic in the sense of being totally immersed in existence in all its corporeality; the ordinary, the banal and the bodily are the playwright's raw materials which he refuses to imbue with any transcendental meaning. But Różewicz's is an unorthodox "realism" unencumbered by illusionistic conventions. Externals, such as plot and cause-and-effect sequentiality, are eliminated in favor of an interior drama that reveals life as it is experienced in the depths of stillness.

To paint a picture of everyday life in which nothing out of the ordinary happens, the author of *The Trap* favors the simplest means: emptiness among events, silence between words, waiting. Action, the most basic element of drama in the traditionalist view, is considered by Różewicz to be the antithesis of realism and thus the negation of true theatre. "My plays have no endings," the Polish poet has declared. Rather than the temporal unfolding of a plot, he strives for the simple duration of a given situation. His aim is the creation of an "open theatre" without fixed perimeters where scenes can be re-ordered or added at will. Różewicz's method of composition is a poetic counterpoint and collage of images producing a polyphonic form capable of accommodating a rich mixture of styles ranging from the colloquial and salacious to elegant parody and pastiche of *fin-de-siècle* fashions and literary traditions.

Questioning the separation of theory from practice, Różewicz has produced a new kind of script that is half treatise and polemic with his predecessors, in which extended stage directions serve as a commentary to interrupt the action and disintegrate the dramatic form. The lengthy stage directions are also arguments with all future directors with whom the playwright may conceivably collaborate. His concept of "open theatre" involves the creation of works that can be completed only in the theatre when director, designer and performers confront the text—and one another.

For Różewicz, the struggle between a play and its realization on stage is the crowning moment of the whole theatrical process. "What I like best in the theatre are the rehearsals," the playwright avows. "When the director fights with everything and everyone. The drama of the battle over the shape of the 'performance'." The texts that Różewicz produces are designed to heighten the conflict by resisting the efforts of theatre artists to dominate the author. "I've written my plays," the author explains, "so as to make difficulties for the directors who stage them, not to make their lives easy."

Różewicz has been fascinated with Kafka ever since he first visited Prague during the Stalin years when the Czech author was forbidden reading. Along with Chekhov and Beckett, Kafka serves as a model for Różewicz's concept of inner drama and directly inspired two of the author's last dramas. *The Hunger Artist*, a highly personal adaptation of Kafka's tale, explores the creative process and the relation of artist to society.

Loosely based on the writer's diaries and letters, *The Trap* is an enigmatic work that "sets traps" for literal-minded critics, directors and audiences. Not one of the Czech author's literary works is ever mentioned (except the generic "Letter to His Father"), nor does the name Kafka once appear. This is hardly the usual life of an artist in which titles and names are constantly dropped. We may ask: is *The Trap* a biographical play about Kafka? Różewicz himself denies that this is the case, insisting that his task as poet, after absorbing masses of facts about the Czech writer, was to depart as far as possible from the documentary material so that his own drama could come into being.

In fact, the Polish author is more concerned with Kafka's inmost fears than with the *realia* of his life, and except for a few fragments from the letters, Różewicz leaves his sources discreetly uncited. *The Trap* dramatizes anxieties and nightmares of the artist Franz as he himself experiences them in relation to his father, his family, his friend, and his fiancée. And despite his attempts to escape the many threats of confinement—existential, societal and historical—assailing him from all sides, the traps are too cunning for Franz.

At first sight the highly fluid structures of time and space that Różewicz has created for *The Trap* make the play seem formless and meandering. The play, however, actually has a firm skeleton of recurring phrases, images and motifs. It is only superficially an "amorphous" play, Różewicz argues, "less like the crown of a tree than the underground roots intertwined and growing in all directions. And therefore the length—in a temporal sense—of a scene on the stage does not always correspond to the length of the duration of that 'scene' or to the space that it occupies in the text."

The playwright uses Tableau XII, "At the Barber's", to illustrate the drama's temporal indeterminacy and elasticity. "The hidden magnitude of that scene is many times greater than what is shown taking place on the stage. It is a scene that comprises the past and the future lurking in the present.... The roots are still hidden in the soil, in the darkness, of the future." The scene takes place in 1914 as war is declared on Serbia, and at the same time the Barber's assistant Vic abuses the Jewish Gentleman like a Nazi thug some twenty years later.

Structured as a series of tableaux, *The Trap* is a family photo album through which we can move backwards and forwards. The central image embodying all the play's dangers, the "trap" is as much biology as history. It is lurking everywhere—as the body in which Franz is imprisoned and as the camp (Auschwitz) to which his sisters will be sent. The "trap" is simultaneously present at all times, in all scenes, extending beyond Franz to the world at large. Throughout the play the Nazis are waiting behind the scenes—represented by the Black Wall. At the denouement of *The Trap*, what has until this point been the tragedy of a family, and of an individual victimized by the family, becomes the tragedy of the Jews. As the actors playing Kafka and his family take their bows, the Executioner-Guards come out from behind the Black Wall that opens at the back of the stage and brutally push the performers off to the trains leaving for the death camps. As the wall closes, only desperate fingers and palms of hands can be seen.

For Jerzy Jarocki, a frequent Różewicz collaborator who directed *The Trap* in 1992, the drama grows out of the confrontation between Kafka's apocalyptic forebodings and Różewicz's own experiences of the war and the Holocaust. Significantly, it is not the sensitive Franz, but his blunt pragmatic Father who scents the coming of the Executioners and forecasts the Holocaust. Franz is too obsessed with the inner concentration camp of creativity to which his art has condemned him to have direct knowledge of the approaching Nazis. Whenever the Executioner-Guards appear, he is in a state of dreaming. Literature, which is Franz's fate, proves perilous to his life.

Built on a poetics of heterogeneity, *The Trap* consists of realistic dialogue, long multi-layered conversations, remembrances, quotations, descriptions, visions, dreams and events taking place outside Franz's consciousness as well as scenes occurring in his presence but not perceived by him. Recurrence and transformation are devices that bind the diverse layers into a whole. Felice's teeth, ready to devour the artist, become the gold crowns of the corpses at the extermination camp Majdanek. The huge wardrobe that for Franz seems a tombstone appears to his Father as a means of salvation in which the family can hide from its persecutors. Father and son pairs occur in different modalities. Despite (or perhaps because of) the writer's instructions to burn his works, Max becomes Franz's "wardrobe" that will preserve his "children" from destruction. Franz's supposed son by Grete is a monster (as he has been for his Father), the revenge of nature on the artist for giving himself exclusively to the creative imagination.

The entire drama is punctuated by the presence of Franz's Animula, or little soul, a childhood double, who, Różewicz tells us in one of his permissive stage directions, may appear at any point throughout the performance. The playwright has written several such appearances into the text, as, for example, in Tableau III where Animula watches Franz's dream of his Father's enactment of Abraham's sacrifice of Isaac, and in Tableau XV where the "little soul" is a silent witness to the deportations through the Black Wall. Never does Animula identify with any of the characters or actions, remaining on stage alone after everyone has gone and leaving the theatre with the last spectator. If the Executioner-Guards take us ahead into a historical future, Animula always brings us back to a timeless past of childhood and its open-eyed perceptions of adult horrors—non-commital, non-judgmental, non-comprehending.

Różewicz is only one of many late twentieth-century playwrights who have found in the Czech author's life and work inspiration for their own dramas, but *The Trap* may well be the most penetrating treatment of Kafka's psychic dilemma. It is curious to note to what extent Różewicz's intensely personal, Polish viewpoint anticipates that of the British writer Alan Bennett, who analyzes Kafka's predicament in almost identical terms, although his own plays on the subject are radically dissimilar.

In his "Author's Note" of 1987 to *Two Kafka Plays* (*Kafka's Dick* and *The Insurance Man*), Bennett views Kafka as a prey to traps both biological and historical. "Death took no chances with Kafka and laid three traps for his life," Bennett writes. "Parched and voiceless from TB of the larynx, he was forty, the victim, as he himself said, of a conspiracy by his own body. But had his lungs not ganged up on him there was a second trap, twenty years down the line when the agents of death would have shunted him, as they did his three sisters, into the gas chambers. That fate, though it was not to be his, is evident in his last photograph. It is a face that prefigures the concentration camp."

The third trap that might have caught Kafka (but never did) is the consequence of Bennett's playful imagining that the Czech writer first avoids TB and then escapes the Nazis by fleeing to America in 1938, only to die of asbestos poisoning which he had contracted in 1917 while managing his brother-in-law's factory. Although Bennett uses the same "trap" metaphor as Różewicz, it is unlikely that the British playwright could have known the Polish drama. And whereas Bennett has written "exterior" drama of a satirical nature about the reception, perception and consumption of Kafka as a cultural artifact in present-day Britain, Różewicz has placed Franz's ambiguous inner drama as son and artist in the context of the tragic historical catastrophe that engulfed his family, his culture, and his civilization.

The ultimate "trap" for Różewicz is Kafka himself, who, the Polish playwright avers, is a "black hole" in the European literary firmament capable of swallowing whatever is attracted to it. In *The Trap* Franz maintains that "Silence contains everything and is more important and vaster than speech and sound." For Różewicz, theatre has great possibilities; there is nothing it cannot encompass. But speaking about silence has become such an impossible task that it has kept him from writing for the stage since 1981.

In 1991—ten years after the play was first published—Różewicz added a prologue to *The Trap* in the form of a poem, "Interrupted Conversation", which is an interior monologue by Franz during the last months or days of his life in a sanatorium near Vienna. Unable to speak, the dying writer communicates with the outside world on scraps of paper. His thoughts are disconnected but return persistently to his obsessions: the various women in his life, his complexes, problems with his Father, reflections on war and death. According to the poet, the prologue offers a summation of the play, with stress on its twin themes of suffering and silence. It is Różewicz's farewell to Kafka.

Daniel Gerould

PROLOGUE

Interrupted conversation

please remove the books
please remove the books

leave the water

Ein Vogel war im Zimmer

I'd rather drink
a glass of white wine
today every sip hurts
like broken glass
cuts my throat
the fire reaches the roof of the mouth
have you touched my lips
does water have lips
I swallow fire

und die Flieder in die Sonne

please don't go I'm not asleep
with eyes closed I can see
faces better the tincture of words
when you all discuss me
in whispers
yesterday my tongue was cotton-wool
today it's quite stiff

after yesterday's conversation with the doctor
between me ill and you
who surround me with love
but are in health
fell a thing we'll not remove
either with love or with words
that thing's my death

Ein Vogel war im Zimmer

PROLOGUE

if only someone had said at least once
Ah! what a light pen you have
or
I admire the inventiveness of your language
what would I think
if a critic were
to enter my room now
and said
I admire the elegance of your language
the inventiveness of thought the specific gravity of the work

now I laugh I'm glad
I'm not allowed to talk

Eine Fliege im Zimmer

Goldregen kann man nicht bekommen?

a huge black fly
hits the window-pane
it's azure-blue in the sun
it hits the window-pane
so I am locked in

when I was a student
I used to kill those heavy
flies on windows-panes
dark-blue full of eggs
she doesn't see the glass
I would kill using a note-book
or the paper I was reading

yellowish-white entrails
oozed out of squashed bodies
I felt sick ready
to vomit
I had to finish one off
twitching on the parapet

und die Flieder in die Sonne

ah! that man wouldn't have killed a fly!
(that's about Emperor Franz-Josef...)

PROLOGUE

let me have a paper
I don't want to sleep
please remove the flowers
they're beautiful but stifling

a fly may enter an open mouth
won't anyone kill that fly
that spitting revolting fly
Musca vomitoria it lands on meat
deposits eggs in places where meat
splits and rots

you live with domestic flies since childhood
you pull off their wings
and bottle them up
musca domestica

in the country at Ottla's I've seen
a beautiful golden fly
called Caesar on a dead mole

sie will wieder zurückkommen!

a fly in the soup that was
an aesthetic and ethical problem
one had to remove it with a spoon
the serving spoons in our house
were heavy silver
maybe silver-plated knives spoons
forks that was father's cold steel
whenever he picked up a spoon a fork
a battle would start at table struggles
with meat and bones
the fly would defend itself
against death one had
to remove it with the tip of the spoon
what's to be done with it where to dump it
mother
would remove the flies from my plate
the soup's flavour would change
I couldn't eat I suspected
father was swallowing the flies
to set us children a good example

PROLOGUE

when I recover I shall write a story
about flies in towns and in the country
about flies on flowers and ceilings
about flies on still lifes
of Dutch painters

alles auch das Bier hat mich gebrannt

I am meat for her
but flies too become ill and die
autumn flies are weak sleepy
in wars men drop down like flies

Zimmerblumen sind ganz anders zu behandeln

I'll go to sleep now

you need to close the sugar-bowl tight
I've seen Pharaoh's ants
they march horizontally they march vertically
towards the sugar-bowl
when I'm better
I'll start reading Forel's
the Swiss myrmecologist's
"Social World of the Ants"
and "The Ants of Switzerland"
the Pharaoh ants survived
all the pharaohs
and Nefretete
(die Schöne kommt)

an ant buried in a pyramid
a subject for a story

Die Ameisen nicht aufessen

I'll never be a book-worm

Ergo bibemus Trinken wir also

Kompott Obst Fruchtsaft
Wasser Fruchtsaft Obst Kompott
Kompott Wasser Fruchtsaft
Wasser Limonade Apfelwein
Obst Wasser
und dabei hatte ich nicht

PROLOGUE

einmal Bier
in a second-hand book-shop
I bought a couple
of old newspapers
"Vossische Zeitung" and "Kriegs-Echo"
August 1914 the outbreak of The Great War
so ten years have passed
an excited screaming crowd on the streets of Prague
Czechs Germans Jews
Jews display the greatest agility
Jewish merchants shout loudest
throughout the whole war
I stood on the side tired amazed
at last I can now read
in peace those old yellowing pages
warum habe ich es im Spital
nicht einmal mit Bier versucht
in old newspapers you can find
all the mistakes and lies
governments and nations will perpetrate
in a year in ten years' time
Totentanz
August 1914
Deutschland einig
Das Ganze Volk hinter dem Kaiser
Wie der Heilige Krieg erklärt wurde
Das Eiserne Kreuz erneut

Sieg auf Sieg! Gott ist mit Euch
und wird auch mit uns sein
Herzlichst drückt
Deine Starke Hand!
Kaiser Franz Joseph
an Kaiser Wilhelm
Wien 24 August

and ah! in the front line
the Tyrtaeus-poet incites to Battle
poor Dehmel and Hauptmann
and the comic Lissauer
poets terrible children

they raise their voices call from the depths
Lissauer's poem *Führer*

PROLOGUE

Dora please copy this
poem a hundred times
and scatter it through the streets of Prague
Vienna and Berlin

sorry that's a joke
read this poem aloud
no! leave it! don't read
of course the poet
also yoked German music
to the war-chariot
patriotism bred monsters
Deutsche Gewehre sollen die Flöten sein
Deutsche Kanonen brummen den Bass darein.
Deutsche Schwerter sind die Geigenbogen,
breit über britische Nacken gezogen
Unsere Kolben trommeln dumpf und hell
auf britischen Fell

wo ist der ewige Frühling?
learn wisdom from folly
learn wisdom from old newspapers
not from text-books learn
history from old newspapers
not from current scripts
lectures the Professor on the rostrum
performs a double somersault
without losing either his glasses or his umbrella
or his beard or his scholarly dignity

, . . . and the prayer of a seven-year old girl
Kätchen Glas aus Danzig

"Ich bitte Dich, Du lieber Gott
Schon unser Volk in Kriegsnot
Siehst Du am Himmel Zeppelin fliegen
So hilf ihm doch, damit wir siegen
Zum Schlusse nimm meinen Dank noch hin,
Das ich ein deutsches Mädchen bin!"

why don't I write poetry
perhaps there's too much light
in the room
but I'm reading
Hölderlin and Eichendorff

PROLOGUE

I read Goethe

Ergo bibemus Trinken wir also
please read this poem
careful don't cut yourself
the glass fell off the table at night
what's happened to the water who carries the flame
the cleaner walks barefoot
might cut
her foot
Darum liebt man
die Wasserjungfrauen

August 1914
Der Kaiser an das deutsche Volk
...So muss den das Schwert entscheiden. Mitten in dem Frieden überfällt uns der Feind. Darum auf! Zu den Waffen. Jedes Schwanken jedes Zögern wäre Verrat am Vaterland...Wir werden uns wehren bis zum letzten Hauch von Mann und Ross...Vorwärts mit Gott, der mit uns sein wird, wie er mit den Vätern war...
Even a German horse would have had a laugh...but the nation stood behind the Kaiser...
And God?

Rhetorische Frage
surely it's
the prince of satans
Beelzebub
in Hebrew:
Baal Zebub
Lord of the flies

post factum

In the spring of 1924 Franz Kafka was dying in the Kierling sanatorium near Vienna. Doctors were advising the patient to avoid conversations; Kafka was a very disciplined patient, he adhered strictly to this instruction and communicated with the aid of notes recorded on slips of paper. Often it was a brief indication, a word or an allusion...His friends supplied 'the rest' which wasn't quite silence. Because of difficulties in swallowing food and drink (Kafka was suffering from tuberculosis of the larynx) the patient was weak and starved like the protagonist of the *Ein Hungerkünstler* story. Kafka was proof-reading this story during the last days of his life. As Dr Robert Klopstock reports, Kafka wept for a long time after finishing with the proofs. The doctor, who together with Dora Diamant looked after the patient right to the end, was shocked by that sobbing because Kafka was a superhumanly self-controlled individual. I conceived the poem *interrupted conversation* as a prologue to *The Trap*. For reasons to do with the theatre (the production) I did not include this text in the play. Now, ten years later, I have decided to complete this "prologue". Many years ago I've had a similar experience with the "prologue" to the play *The Funny Old Man*, which had an existence independent of the play until it turned into an epilogue and grew into the organism of the play. Will the same happen to the poem *interrupted conversation*? I don't know. The *Gesprächblätter* contain several dozen notes selected by Max Brod. In writing the "prologue" I made use of only ten short notes (sentences?). I found it difficult to articulate this prologue (this poem?); after fifty years of composing poetry and plays I came to understand the futility of unravelling the Franz Kafka "mystery". My only justification is that I worked and wrote as best I could. The fact that I am justifying myself maybe demonstrates the irreversible collapse of so-called "belles-lettres", especially of "poetry". This is my farewell to Franz Kafka. I'm 69. The time of farewells is close.

THE CHARACTERS

ANIMULA	FRANZ
JOSIE	FATHER
MOTHER	OTTLA
ELLI	VALLI
	FELICE
MAX	GRETE
COBBLER	ZENEK
BARBER	VIC
EXECUTIONERS	SALESMAN
GENTLEMAN	WAITRESS

ANIMULA

Throughout the performance FRANZ'S little soul may appear on stage. The soul may be played by a little girl in a white dress. The soul sits in the corner, sometimes it gives the impression of listening, of noticing everything, and at times it appears blind, absent. ANIMULA takes no interest in FRANZ or his thoughts, feelings, sufferings and joys which it doesn't share. It takes no interest, no part in his life, and it has no role in his physical or intellectual development. When the performance is over and all the characters are gone, ANIMULA remains on the stage alone.

TABLEAU I

A servant's room

A small room with a skylight. A bed piled high with eiderdowns and pillows stacked on top of each other. Against the wall a large wooden chest decorated with flowers and birds. Above the bed "holy pictures", painted brightly on glass, representing the Mother of God, the Sacred Heart of Jesus and St. George fighting the dragon. A rug on the floor, a stool with a wash-basin, and above, a small mirror and dried garlands and herbs. The room is whitewashed and very clean. A fat, pretty girl of about thirty is sitting on the stool; she is wearing thick woollen socks, and she is darning a stocking. A thin black-haired boy of about six is sitting on the chest. He is holding a saucer full of honey which he scoops with a small spoon and then pours back onto the saucer, watching the golden thread.

JOSIE. Well, my little one, is the honey nice?
FRANZ. I am afraid...I am afraid...
JOSIE. And what are you afraid of? I am here.
FRANZ. I am afraid of daddy...daddy said he'll tear me apart like a frog.
JOSIE. Daddy is having you on...mothers and fathers don't harm their children because they love them.
FRANZ. But I am afraid of daddy, he grinds his teeth when he looks at me and his hands move like a crab's and my honey turns sour.
JOSIE. The Lord said you must honour your father and mother. Don't be afraid Franzie, as soon as we hear your daddy's steps I'll hide you under the eiderdown or in the chest. Does the honey taste better now?
FRANZ. A little.
JOSIE. There you are!
FRANZ. Because the frogs...
JOSIE. And what did you do to the frogs? Children are real torturers.
FRANZ. Charles showed us; he tore a frog apart and the guts came out. Ottla burst into tears and started hitting Felix but I ran away...Charles said you can fit a straw into a frog's behind and blow it up so it changes into a dragon and flies away!
JOSIE. Felix is an idiot! One day the master will give him such a hiding!
FRANZ. And how do you give people a hiding?
JOSIE. Eat the honey.
FRANZ. And how do you give people a hiding?
JOSIE. Come over here and I'll show you!

THE TRAP

FRANZ. And this honey you brought from home, is it straight from a hive? Yesterday daddy said to me: expect honey from bees but a child only pees.
JOSIE. But of course!
FRANZ. And how many beehives do you have in the country?
JOSIE. I've told you a hundred times—three.
FRANZ. And what are they like?
JOSIE. One is like a bear standing on his hind legs, another has the shape of St. Florian.
FRANZ. And the third is like a barrel, and in their tummies they all have bees with one queen. And the drones? What about the drones?
JOSIE. They are just like you.
FRANZ. *(Licks clean the saucer and runs to JOSIE).* Lick me, see how sweet I am!
JOSIE. *(Kisses him firmly on both cheeks and then wipes his face with her hand).* Oh my thin one! Run away now—if your daddy sees you now he'll tear you like a frog!
FRANZ. *(Holding up his hands in prayer).* Let me stay here a little longer. It smells so nice here. Haven't you got children of your own?
JOSIE. Well, no.
FRANZ. Why? *(JOSIE swipes her hand as if chasing a fly).* You'll give birth to a calf.
JOSIE. What nonsense!
FRANZ. Yes, a calf, cows have calves.
JOSIE. But I'm not a cow!
FRANZ. Daddy shouts at you, you cow, you old cow, stop mooing. I heard it, I heard you mooing.

(JOSIE puts the darning aside)

I don't love daddy, he shouts at you and he shouts horribly at Valli, and he gnashes his teeth at me.
JOSIE. You must honour your father and mother. This is the commandment.
FRANZ. Whose commandment?
JOSIE. God's commandment.
FRANZ. That God to whom you pray?
JOSIE. Yes.
FRANZ. Is God over there?

(Points to one of the pictures)

JOSIE. That is the Lord Jesus.
FRANZ. And why is the Lord Jesus hanging on a cross and God isn't?
JOSIE. Because evil men have tortured and crucified Jesus.
FRANZ. But why?
JOSIE. For our sins and for our salvation.

TABLEAU I

FRANZ. I know that people have tortured and crucified Jesus but he is lying!
JOSIE. Who is lying? What kind of talk is that?
FRANZ. Theo told me they learn about confession and communion and that he knows everything...

(Runs up to JOSIE, snuggles up to her and hides his head against her knees)

I never tortured Jesus, I didn't kill him...

(Bursts into tears and repeats crying)

I didn't kill Jesus...I didn't...only evil Jews did it.
JOSIE. *(Comforts the boy in her arms, strokes his head, rocks and kisses him. Gradually the boy grows quiet).* Don't cry...come I'll wash your eyes, otherwise mummy will know you've been crying.

(Leads the boy to the basin, washes his face with her hand and dries it with a clean white towel)

FRANZ. *(Smiling at JOSIE).* But Theo was saying...that I...that we...
JOSIE. *(Stroking the boy's face).* Go, go run around in the yard.

(Slaps his behind, FRANZ runs out laughing)

TABLEAU II

Years later

A dining table with a flowery lampshade above. Dark heavy furniture. The table is covered with a cloth. A family supper is in progress. FRANZ and OTTLA lean towards each other, whisper and stifle giggles.

FATHER. Silence at table! *(A sound of laughter)*. Isn't it enough that that cow messed up the food... why is that girl laughing... well, tell me, why are you laughing?! And your little brother... always silent and gloomy... well, tell father what you are talking about?! Talking about me I'm sure! I slave away all day to feed a whole bunch of layabouts and I'm not even allowed to eat in peace. Time and again I have told you that a table is where you eat and there is no room for giggling and chattering. This soup is pure swill!
MOTHER. *(Quietly)*. I'm sorry, Hermann.
FATHER. *(Calmly)*. It is I who crave forgiveness, Julia, on account of your children.

(FATHER leans over his plate, guzzling)

Naturally Franz does not like it, his palate is too delicate. At his age I was glad to have a plate of potatoes! I never had soups, bouillons, broths, chicken, meat... I was ten when I started working and so it remained until this day. But who cares? The lords and ladies in our house lounge about and wait for choice morsels to fall into their mouths. Franz! If you don't like our company you may leave.
FRANZ. Father, I...
FATHER. *(Banging the table with his fists)*. Silence when I am talking to you! "I...I...I..." All he can say is "I...I" and what are you? What? Nothing. And don't you dare talk to me as if I were your snivelling little friend. I am not your friend. Look at the face he is making! Have I hurt your feelings?! I can't even utter a few words in my own home. I don't demand from you either love or family feelings because you are incapable of them. Well, why aren't you all eating? Why is everybody staring? As man eats, so he works.

(A servant brings in meat, potatoes and gravy, eyeing the master of the house nervously)

Their lordships are sitting and are condescending to eat. When I was seven I had to stand whole days pushing barrow-loads of potatoes or fuel. I used to get so tired I would fall asleep at table, not like you lot, each in their own beds on a mattress under an eiderdown. There were eight of us, we all slept in the same room and we three boys in the same bed.

MOTHER. I'm sorry, Hermann.

(Signals the maid to leave the room)

FATHER. *(Takes a long time to serve himself meat and potatoes from a dish which he then passes towards his wife. FRANZ pushes his own plate away, OTTLA starts eating with relish. FATHER eats quickly, cutting large portions of meat, and occasionally removing gristle and bone from his teeth. The other children eat in silence.)*

Oh yes, one used to be happy in those days if one could get one's fill of potatoes and pasta. None of us pushed a plate full of food away. We would take turns at wearing out the clothes and shoes and the wind was cold on the backsides.

(FATHER takes a bone which he begins to pick. His black moustache with its tips trained upwards rises above the bone, his teeth gleam. He has a napkin round his neck which he uses frequently to wipe his fingers and moustache. MOTHER touches FRANZ'S forehead with her hand—it is a delicate, frightened gesture which, however, has not escaped FATHER'S attention who stops picking the bone, throws it on his plate, spattering the table with gravy and potatoes.)

He probably thinks he is ill because he doesn't like the food. Those who are ill should stay in bed, people who sit at table are well. He is fussing: why don't you cut his meat and feed him? At his age I had to join the business as a messenger-boy and then as a younger assistant. Nobody stroked my forehead although now and again the boss would put a flea in my ear! Ha! Ha! Ha!

(Bursts into laughter)

Clown! People who think only about themselves, exclusively about themselves, about their stomach and their intestines and their digestion, they have no time to take an interest either in their brothers and sisters or in their parents. Julia, don't neglect yourself, you haven't eaten a thing yet. Don't take any notice of them, I assure you that when we are old they won't even give us a glass of water.

(ELLI who is sitting at the corner of the table begins to weep. FATHER, folding his napkin)

TABLEAU II

And what is she up to? She'll drown everything in those tears.
MOTHER. Hermann, there is still the pudding.
ELLI. *(In a quiet voice interrupted by sobbing).* I...uncle...I...nothing...
FATHER. Ottla! Eat with your mouth shut.

(Pulls out a toothpick from his pocket and meticulously begins to clean his teeth, clearing out bits of meat and looking about him with satisfaction. He surveys the family like an owner and returns to picking his teeth. MOTHER strokes FRANZ'S hand under the table while he sits with his head bowed. OTTLA eats her pudding very carefully, leans over towards FRANZ and whispers in his ear. FATHER scratches his ear with the toothpick.)

So!

(Leans over slightly towards MOTHER)

Perhaps you should rest a little?

(Pats the chubby VALLI on her cheek and leaves the room, his shoes squeaking. Silence. ELLI gets up and leaves. There is growing hubbub and laughter around the table. The maid is clearing the dishes helped by OTTLA.)

MOTHER. *(To FRANZ).* My son...
FRANZ. Yes, mummy?
MOTHER. Are you ill, don't you feel well?
FRANZ. No, mummy.
MOTHER. Why weren't you eating, perhaps you'll eat it later? Josie will bring it to your room.
FRANZ. No thank you, mummy. May I leave the table?

(MOTHER kisses him and watches him leave in his black uniform)

OTTLA. May I eat your pudding?

(FRANZ takes out two matches from a box and begins to pick his ears, and then opens his mouth wide like a hippopotamus cleaning his teeth...parodying his father.)

MOTHER. Please stop it, it's disgusting!

(VALLI laughs compulsively and convulsively. OTTLA and the maid continue to clear the dishes. OTTLA returns, sweeps the crumbs off the table-cloth and places a vase with artificial flowers on the table.)

FRANZ. Valli! You laugh like a chimp!

VALLI. Mother!

FRANZ. Today I have eaten so many potatoes that my happiness has no bounds. Had our distinguished head of the family received such a portion of potatoes free he would have been the happiest of men in this vale of tears. There's children's gratitude for you!

MOTHER. Franz! Don't speak in that tone about your father, it is very unpleasant.

FRANZ. *Ich lebe im Saus und Braus! Meine Damen und Herren! Im Saus und Maus und Braus...*

(Kisses Mother's hand and leaves)

TABLEAU III

A dream
A sacrificial animal

FRANZ is lying asleep on top of his bed. He is dressed in a black suit with a white shirt and tie. FATHER is sharpening two knives at a table with a dish and some plates. The table is grey, small, without legs, somewhat like an altar composed of flat stones. A beam of light falls from a black emptiness above. FRANZ'S ANIMULA is collecting firewood which it places around the table.

ANIMULA. Daddy, do I have to collect more sticks?

(FATHER sharpens the knives in silence)

Where is the sacrificial lamb?
FATHER. *(Stands up and looks huge)*. You are the sacrificial lamb.

(Approaches FRANZ with a rope, holds him, covers his face with his hands. Ties his hands and feet and fingers his neck. Picks up the knife and touches the boy's neck with it.)

FRANZ. *(Waking up with a cry and then, in the darkness, a sound like sobbing. FRANZ talks to FATHER through a vast darkness)*. Father, so it is only blood, my death which can change and mollify you? You hate me, but why? I am afraid that people will begin shouting at me, will stamp their feet and pull my ears like a little boy's. Father, I am afraid, I am sweating all over, my palms are moist, damp. I wish to be your child, I can see I am weak, I am falling apart, I am falling apart, I am afraid of people, I am afraid of you, I am afraid of little girls who are malicious little monkeys. I am a dirty animal...

TABLEAU IV

A furniture store

FRANZ. A wardrobe.

(Inspecting wardrobe)

We'll buy a wardrobe...a wardrobe! A strange word.

(Smiles)

FELICE. We must buy a three-door wardrobe for clothes, a cupboard for bed clothes, two bedside tables, two beds or a double-bed and a linen cupboard.
FRANZ. Wardrobes. Drawers. So we are buying a wardrobe?!

(Surprised)

Felice, do we really need these wardrobes and cupboards?
FELICE. We must decide. If it is not to be this wardrobe, then perhaps that other one, but we mustn't make an exhibition of ourselves. Wardrobes seem to frighten you. You don't think I'm going to lock up a 36-year-old insurance agent and writer in a wardrobe? Two wardrobes and two bedside tables in the bedroom, and possibly a cupboard in the kitchen, a cupboard in your room, a cupboard or a shelf for books, a cupboard in the hall, a table, two tables, three tables, a little table, a tiny table, a stool, a wardrobe, a little cupboard, a chest of drawers, a wardrobe with drawers...

(Her mouth opens faster and wider and FRANZ notices her shining golden teeth)

FRANZ. We don't need a wardrobe or a chair, we don't need anything, anyway in my room there is a table, sofa, a chair, a bookshelf, that's all. Surely you don't imagine me sleeping in a shared bedroom under the same bedclothes, in the same bed. At night I work! Even the breathing of a loved one is like an engine roar. Listen, let's leave the wardrobes and the beds, that's not the point. I'm sorry, *(Glances at his silver pocket watch)* I have to go.
FELICE. *(Is absorbed in inspecting a wardrobe, opening and shutting its drawers).* I have reserved an hour to look for our furniture—ours of course because after all they are mine too, both the wardrobe and the table.

THE TRAP

(Smiles, taking her fiancé by the arm)

Why all this struggle with a wardrobe? Did that piece of furniture ever cause you any harm? Naturally, I don't insist on this wardrobe although I find it difficult to imagine a home without wardrobes. We aren't nomads.
FRANZ. *(Seriously)*. You'll be living with me, not with a wardrobe.
FELICE. *(Smiling)*. That's what I expect, but the lady of the house, the hostess, must have cupboards and wardrobes.
FRANZ. If a chair or a wardrobe is to be the basis of our relationship then I can't see...I must...I think I am a little feverish...I have to go now...I have no relationship with furniture. I have no wish to become a prisoner, a slave, I can't bear a wardrobe on my shoulders...maybe that's my cross? A wardrobe.

(The salesman who has been hovering around the couple, now listens with increasing amazement. Another young couple enters the store. They look excited, the salesman moves towards them.)

FELICE. *(Squeezing FRANZ'S arm)*. My dear, people are looking at us. Let's leave that wardrobe in peace, I'll come here tomorrow with Ottla and we shall choose a wardrobe which you are sure to like. I want to buy furniture which you too will like...
FRANZ. Everything you buy will...if they please you then I too...so in a word...then I absolutely...
FELICE. That's how you are talking now, dear, but later? If I were to choose on my own a three-door walnut wardrobe I am sure you would be miserable...and instead of looking at me you would be looking at the wardrobe! With dislike or maybe even hatred...in the end you would run away from this wardrobe...or rather you would run away from me.
FRANZ. *(Smiling, bows and kisses FELICE'S hand)*. I am sorry I have a bit of a headache. So, all right, let's decide.
FELICE. The bedroom suite looks pretty, don't you think?

(Meanwhile the other young pair are inspecting beds. They smile at each other and whisper. The young woman gently prods her man's arm)

FRANZ. *(Mumbling)*. Disgusting...

(Moves over to the other side of the showroom as though he wished to hide in the corner. FELICE is now alone, she then moves towards FRANZ and they talk together. FELICE is irritated and angry. FRANZ stands before her like a scolded pupil. FELICE goes over to the salesman, talks to him, he nods his head and a moment later produces a tray with a glass of water. FRANZ takes some of the pills out of his pocket and swallows them drinking the water. Meanwhile the other young pair move over to inspect the cupboards and ward-

TABLEAU IV

robes which they open and examine very carefully, counting the hangers and opening the drawers. FRANZ approaches them from behind, observing the wardrobe. He has now forgotten about FELICE who is talking to the salesman. Removal-men enter. They are bare-chested, their shoulders covered in belts and ropes. The saleman points to the wardrobe and the men prepare to remove it. Their huge muscular bodies and red faces are in sharp contrast to the elegantly dressed customers. Their muscles move beneath taut skins producing different reactions in the ladies and the men. Only the salesman has his whole attention focussed on the wardrobe to ensure that the men cause no damage. The men leave followed by the young couple. FRANZ and FELICE are left alone in silence.)

FRANZ. *(With simulated animation).* Felice, have you read the little book I gave you last month?

(Engrossed in her thoughts she doesn't hear, or perhaps pretends she doesn't hear. Walks over to a double-bed, takes off her gloves, slowly, thoughtfully, strokes the bedstead with her hand.)

Felice!
FELICE. *(Raises her head, looks puzzled at FRANZ as though he were a stranger).* We'll take this double-bed. This whole suite, the mirror, the drawers, the chests, the armchairs, the dressing table, the fur rug to go by the bed. Your mother has given us a splendid green plush bedspread—it just fits the double-bed. Your mother and my mother have formed a little conspiracy.
FRANZ. Felice!
FELICE. I am sorry.
FRANZ. My love, I was asking you whether you had read the *Kreutzer Sonata* which I gave you last month.
FELICE. *(Uncertain).* Yes...I don't remember...there is so much work in the office...perhaps I did start it...I don't know, I must have put it somewhere...surely it's nothing urgent?! Must I read it here, now, at once? We'll take it with us, we'll have a whole month, our honeymoon.
FRANZ. So you haven't even opened the book.
FELICE. I'll read it today and tomorrow. I'll give you a full account of it.
FRANZ. If you don't wish to, don't bother reading it. Anyway you have your own favourite authors. Why didn't you tell me about the bedspread? Why didn't you show it to me? I am not sure it is practical. I'm not sure double-beds have special virtues. Maybe they had for our grandparents and don't forget that because of the nature of my work I need a sofa in my study. Can't you see that? After all, you know what work I do.
FELICE. I know my dear, I know everything and I remember everything, don't worry I won't eat you!

(Suddenly FELICE bursts into laughter showing a huge row of teeth. She laughs freely and fully so that her gums and tongue as well as her teeth are visible. FRANZ is staring at her, into her damp open mouth cavity at the rows of teeth and

the mobile tongue. FELICE is still laughing when the salesman returns to the shop. She pulls out a lace handkerchief from her handbag and dries her eyes. FRANZ looks thoughtfully at FELICE who takes no notice of him, goes over to a mirror, looks at herself and adjusts her hat.)

Don't worry, we'll ask Ottla to alter that cover...
FRANZ. What cover?
FELICE. Ottla will simply cut the bedspread in half and bind the edges. She is marvellous with her hands. Don't worry the tiniest bit. We shall have two covers, two beds and between us we'll have this magnificent mirror.

(To the salesman)

What's inside the mattresses? Aren't they a bit hard?
SALESMAN. They are stuffed with seaweed.

(Pressing the mattress with his hand)

The lady and gentleman may like to try! It's very elastic and at the same time quite incredibly cuddly.
FELICE. Don't you want to try?

(FELICE sits down hard on the bed, the springs can be heard jangling. FRANZ remains silent. Enjoying herself, she bounces on the bed and eventually collapses on her back stretching her arms towards FRANZ.)

Lift me, I'm sorry! Help me.

(Still laughing, she then raises herself without help, grows serious, and turns to the salesman.)

I am very... in fact this is our second engagement... my fiancé... that is, we both of us are getting the apartment ready, furnishing it... I am in a terrible state... I've never made such important purchases, after all, buying furniture is not like buying gloves.
SALESMAN. Our firm's furniture are objects which serve not only our customers, but their children and grandchildren. You may be as certain of them as of your happy marriage. If the gentleman is not at this moment able to decide regarding these pieces of furniture, I invite you both to our showroom in a fortnight's time when we shall have the most fashionable designs from the Viennese firm of Thonet.
FELICE. My fiancé is not well today so let's put it off until next month. Thank you very much.

(FELICE shakes the salesman's hand and moves through the door. FRANZ puts on his hat. They leave. The SALESMAN looks puzzled and taps his forehead.)

TABLEAU V

Parents

The parents' bedroom. Twin beds side by side. Night tables. A what-not covered with albums and papers.

FATHER. Never a good word. I never heard anything beyond the mumbled "thank you," the conventional courtesies in a restaurant or at a barber's... nothing else. Not a shadow of affection or interest. The home is where you eat, relieve yourself and sleep. They like you so long as you fuss around them. No! You don't see anything because you love them. I am an old fool, don't listen to this silly chatter.

(Goes over to his wife's bed, sits on the edge and takes her hand)

MOTHER. They're not bad...they...
FATHER. They are totally indifferent to me, as if I were a stranger, an old shoe. Take Franz—he never comes up to me, never smiles...he sits there puffed up, always nursing some slight. For twenty years I have slaved for him like an ox, like the worst animal! He looks at me blankly, his lips tight. At times he'll murmur something, God knows what. But for outsiders there are smiles, courtesies, books, theatre tickets.
MOTHER. Perhaps it is our fault?
FATHER. So it is your fault they don't love us. After all, they have turned you into a servant and me into a working ox. I think they want to finish us off.
MOTHER. But they are good children! They love us very much.
FATHER. They love us the way parasites love the organism on which they feed, like fleas on a dog.
MOTHER. Don't talk like that, these are our children...I...

(Turns her head towards the wall)

FATHER. You alone...they'll go away...anyway they were never with us.
MOTHER. Franz.
FATHER. About him I don't...I can't listen to this...he isn't a grown man, he is...I just don't understand! That wretched engagement, that fiancée...if I were Felice I would throw him downstairs.
MOTHER. Well, he is a writer, an artist, Max told me Franz is a great writer.

FATHER. Max is a great piss-pot, with sweaty palms and feet...they all have sweaty palms and feet...it's disgusting...when I shake Max's hand I have to wipe mine afterwards. I know Franz is writing something. I haven't read it, I am too simple to understand what his lordship deigns to compose in the middle of the night. Of course I have read Goethe, I have read Raabe...they too are writers...maybe even greater than Max and Franz...somehow I understood all they said...here nothing—it's like eating paper.

MOTHER. But if you showed just a little interest...said a kind word.

FATHER. That isn't bread, that isn't a profession. How can an insurance agent...I won't pretend to lie to you or me...that's not in my character. As far as I'm concerned his writing is not worth the paper it's written on. I once asked Felice what she thought of Franz's books. She smiled and said nothing.

MOTHER. Sometimes I am so tired...I'd like to fall asleep, my dear, to have a rest.

FATHER. I've exhausted you with this chatter...

(Bends over his wife and tucks the eiderdown around her)

Go to sleep, I'll sit here for a while, perhaps I'll read you something...you always fall asleep when I read aloud. Don't worry.

(Strokes his wife's head, she kisses his hand and turns to the wall)

TABLEAU VI

To the rescue—a hotel room

FELICE. Whenever you are drowning you grab anything that's at hand—a waitress, let it be a waitress... a kitchen maid at home, that's all right too... a doctor's receptionist, splendid... I the wife will always be at hand, that's best but may be awkward, so you choose my friend Grete. So you write two letters and propose to Grete and me at once. Best of all the first one that turns up, so long as she isn't a prostitute because that's unhygienic and little Franz is afraid of venereal diseases and of his father. Sometimes when I look at you with love I feel like vomiting you and myself... "Help! Help!" you cry, "I am drowning, I am dying, I am in a terrible state"... we all come running... Mother, Ottla, the kitchen maid, all your "women" and I like a fool... only your Father who knows you like a bad coin grins beneath that moustache and waits... and he is right to wait... the water has hardly reached your knees and you cry that it's pouring into your mouth. Mother nearly died of fright... I had to leave work... three telegrams in three hours! Oh yes, you had a headache! But does the whole world have to know about it? Well! Tell me why I came here. Why did I rush to this hotel bedroom, so what do you want from me? Do you know yourself what you want, what you will want tomorrow, in a week's time, in a day's time, in an hour?

(FELICE takes off her coat and drapes it over a chair. She is wearing a simple skirt, a short-sleeved lace blouse and a little hat or beret. FRANZ is stretched out on the bed in black trousers, waistcoat, white shirt, dark tie and black patent leather shoes. His feet rest on a newspaper, his "best" jacket hangs on a chair. FELICE takes off her hat, goes to the mirror, adjusting and pinning up her splendid mane of thick black hair. She is holding hairpins in her teeth, her arms raised high to reveal hairy armpits.)

I wish no part in this comedy, I am not an actress or an artiste, I am a clerk, I am thirty, I wish to get married, to create a home for my chosen man, bear children, live with him for some fifteen to twenty years, die before him or bury him, that is my whole philosophy. I have never pretended to be either a nymph or a sphinx. Once already you have made a right fool of me, I was a laughing stock and you were an idiot, an infantile idiot. Well, here I am, I have arrived... I can see you are alive, lolling in bed and unwilling to talk, and there was I taking you to buy furniture, curtains, pots and pans, washbasins and kitchen cloths. I am sure you enjoyed yourself hugely watching my activities.

FRANZ. Don't let go of me...I haven't the strength...my body disgusts me, inside I feel how everything rots and falls apart...

FELICE. I haven't come to arrange a funeral...are you afraid? Are you afraid of me? How can I help you? I know you don't need my brain, my intelligence, my knowledge or my soul...all you need is my body...you don't even need my name and surname...yes...it wouldn't matter if I were Grete, Milena, Vlasta, Else...any girl so long as she had...so what is it? Here I am! This body has travelled 500 kilometers to reach you...it tossed about in a stuffy compartment...I have brought it here because it may save you...I will wash this body...yes, just one minute...now this body will enter your bed...and now what else? Well, speak...but make it quick because the body will get bored and go away.

FRANZ. You are life itself, my life...you're agitated.

(FELICE goes out to the bathroom and returns in a moment, walks over to the mirror. Dabs perfume on her forehead, her neck, behind the ears and sits on the bed)

FELICE. Here you are, eat me...eat my body, eat the meat...I brought it in a dish, all prepared. All you have to do is open your mouth...can't you understand I am a woman?

FRANZ. I am ill...today blood gushed out of my throat and nose...I wished to tell you I am spitting blood...I wanted to say goodbye. This illness was concealed. Doctors give me a year or two. So you see, Felice, there won't be any wardrobes or beds, or children, or nappies, or potties...I wanted to say "sorry" and "goodbye." You see I am moving into the other world...don't touch me.

(Voices and a waltz tune drift from below)

You must be hungry. Shall we go downstairs?

(FELICE sits motionless)

Or would you like dinner ordered here?

FELICE. So he found a way out after all.

FRANZ. Are you talking to me?

FELICE. I was talking to myself.

FRANZ. I've booked the next room along...you'll be able to rest.

FELICE. He'd rather have an illness than me...

FRANZ. It's so good you're here...I'll ring for the waiter and order the supper.

TABLEAU VI

(Goes up to FELICE and puts his hand on her head)

Will you stay?
FELICE. And yet he's escaped.

(FRANZ drops his hand, moves to the door, presses the bell. FELICE gets up, looks in the mirror and tidies her hair. FRANZ puts on his jacket and stands next to FELICE...puts his arm around her...they stand as though posing for a photograph...sound of the waltz tune.)

FRANZ. You can have a steak and I'll have an omelette, we'll have fruit salad, wine, cake and coffee.

(FELICE embraces FRANZ, hides her face and holds him tightly)

Wait, I've forgotten the name of that cake. You had it in Budapest, you were greedy like a child, your mouth full, your cheeks...
FELICE. Since you haven't died...since you aren't dying...surely we don't discuss cakes when we are dying...my presence here...you don't need me, not even in the next room.

(FELICE looks around)

Here you have everything to make you happy: table, light, loneliness.

(A wiry, energetic, cheerful waitress comes in)

WAITRESS. You rang, sir.

(Pulls out a notebook in readiness)

FRANZ. A dinner for two. Yes...well...no soup, no extras...something basic...a steak, fried potatoes, a salad and then an omelette with spinach...perhaps a fruit salad, a cake...you know...the Hungarian cake...dark on the outside, light inside...but I don't know what it's called...the chef will know, it's a famous cake...Rosé wine, coffee and mineral water.

(The WAITRESS smiles and takes down the order. FELICE silently watches the WAITRESS and FRANZ. The WAITRESS leaves smiling. FRANZ looks at FELICE.)

FELICE. I am leaving. I am neither hungry nor tired...in fact...thank you...don't escort me, don't take any trouble and don't write to me. I am grown up and I won't get lost at the station or in the train. Don't send me telegrams or girlfriends—just do this for me: leave me alone.

FRANZ. Have I... may we shake hands.
FELICE. *(Gives him her hand, then picks up her bag and suitcase).* Please don't bother coming... the suitcase is light...
FRANZ. *(He is now alone in the room. He stands motionless then pulls out his handkerchief and carefully dries his hands and lies down on the sofa).*

    I wanted to prove myself, to demonstrate strength of will, to delay writing to you until I had finished the first act, but the room is empty, no one bothers about me. It's as if they said to themselves: leave him alone, can't you see he is absorbed in his own affairs, he is completely oblivious of the world. And so in the end, man, that old rat, digs new passageways. Yes, that wardrobe, it will undoubtedly cause our first and last quarrel. I will say, "Let's throw it away." You will say, "Leave it!" I will say, "Choose between the wardrobe and me." You will say, "Agreed," and will slowly descend the stairs...

TABLEAU VII

Courting

A black wall covered with posters and advertisements, shop signs of a pub, a barber and a shoemaker. Occasional passers-by walk along the wall in the light of an invisible street light. A fat young girl in a pink sweater, high-heeled leather shoes and a beret, walks along, followed at a short distance by two men. They talk, looking at the girl's behind, at her legs covered in flesh-coloured silk stockings with seams. The girl and the men appear against the wall, pass along, disappear and re-appear. The men stop outside the barber's.

FRANZ. Have you discovered where she lives? What's her name?
MAX. Her name is Slovik.
FRANZ. Slovik?
MAX. Jana Slovik, she lives with her family, her father is a cobbler...
FRANZ. She is the daughter of a cobbler... a cobbler! Do you know, father used to threaten me when I was a little boy that he would make me a cobbler's apprentice. "We'll apprentice him to a cobbler," he used to say to Mother, and there was fear in her eyes and a faint smile. So she's a cobbler's daughter and lives with her family.
MAX. Yes, she lives with her family. I was there last week, I took a pair of shoes to be mended and I am supposed to have them back tomorrow.
FRANZ. You're as crafty as Mephisto.
MAX. At your service, doctor.
FRANZ. So she does have a family.
MAX. And you thought she'd jumped out of your head or the sea spray, that she has no father, mother, grandpa on her father's side and a granny on the mother's side. Like you she has brothers, sisters, cousins, aunts and uncles.
FRANZ. Keep to the subject, my friend.
MAX. I am collecting my shoes tomorrow. You may come with me. This, in fact, seems to me absolutely necessary if you have serious intentions towards the girl. You'll meet daddy and mummy and the other children, and you'll have a clearer picture.
FRANZ. Of course, there's always a father... and mother of course... and brothers and sisters.
MAX. You seem constantly surprised by this strange phenomenon. The world is so constructed that even a doctor has a mother and father who bore him and also has brothers and sisters.

FRANZ. *(Thoughtfully).* Yes. Even Jesus.
MAX. He had family problems.
FRANZ. I've often thought about that problem...
MAX. I know, you are, you were, and you will be alone...but Miss Slovik has a large family.
FRANZ. So she's got a father. And what about those brothers and sisters? Are there many?
MAX. I've even counted them. Apart from Jana, who is the eldest, there seem to be another ten, or at least nine offspring of different ages from a suckling baby right up to teenagers and youths.
FRANZ. Ten of them!
MAX. Maybe only nine, I could have got it wrong, they kept crawling out of different corners.
FRANZ. And how many girls?
MAX. Five I think, six with Jana.
FRANZ. And what's the house like?
MAX. They live in a basement, in two rooms. The first room is used as a workshop while in the second they have their bedroom and kitchen, though I think the kitchen is in an alcove behind a curtain. I've no idea where the bathroom is, as for the toilet, use your imagination.
FRANZ. Thank you.
MAX. Pleased to be of help. I must admit that this family nest is comparatively neat and clean. In the window of the workshop facing the street there are potted geraniums and a white curtain. Despite the early hour the head of the family appeared to be slightly tipsy. He is not a conversationalist, but is courteous and sensible.
FRANZ. When are you collecting those shoes?
MAX. Are you coming with me?
FRANZ. *(Embracing MAX).* I'd like to ask you...
MAX. I refuse.
FRANZ. It's a matter of life and death for me.
MAX. I can't.
FRANZ. This is my last wish, the last request of a condemned man.
MAX. No.

(Frees himself from FRANZ'S embrace, takes off his glasses and polishes them)

FRANZ. This is my only chance to return to life... *Ich friere und starre in dem Winter, der mich umgibt...*
MAX. What role have you given me?
FRANZ. Are you angry?
MAX. No. I'm listening.
FRANZ. I'd like you to prepare the ground. I can't go with you into their basement and ask for the hand of the eldest daughter while you collect your shoes. Can you imagine that?

MAX. This is not an engagement so I don't imagine anything.
FRANZ. I can't ask for her hand in that crowd of brats.
MAX. Why not?
FRANZ. The mother may just be doing the washing, the father may be drunk. If only Jana lived alone...
MAX. In a summerhouse. Instead there is a teeming family. If only maidens grew on trees! A fruit ripening and turning red, eventually falling into the lap without mummy and daddy, six little sisters and seven brothers... each brother with his own problems.
FRANZ. But I can't just walk in there and ask for a blessing.
MAX. Precisely. When I was there they were cooking cabbage. When the smell of boiling cabbage hits you, you'll run away!
FRANZ. I'll get engaged and married despite the cabbage!
MAX. You react extremely violently to all smells. I recall that the smell of boiling cauliflower stopped you asking for the hand of a Swiss girl.
FRANZ. *(Smiling)*. I am beginning to suspect you are in league with my father—you are his agent.

(MAX takes off his glasses and observes his friend with a short-sighted look)

You must prepare the ground for my arrival.
MAX. I am not worthy, Oh Lord!
FRANZ. During a casual, uncommitted chat, you will tell old Slovik that you have a good friend, a bachelor, a clerk with a good salary...who fancies his daughter Jana. You can also say that your friend has a large apartment which is furnished...yes, furnished.
MAX. A furnished apartment.
FRANZ. You will tell him that my intentions are serious and I wish to pay the parents an official visit. Depending on the parents' reaction you may hint at an early engagement. I am pressed for time, you understand, so I am giving you full powers of attorney, you may even fix the engagement date. In other words, you have a free hand—this time I don't wish to postpone the wedding.
MAX. Jana is a dishwasher. She is not a waitress, she is not a barmaid, she is simply a dishwasher.
FRANZ. You tell me what I know already. Jana washes dishes. That is more useful than writing bad books or painting awful pictures and it's less harmful than writing newspaper articles. A carpenter, a gardener, a cobbler...
MAX. *(Irritated)*. Your're bluffing! We nobodies write to buy bread and shoes.
FRANZ. *Im Leben ein einziges gutes Buch geschrieben zu haben ist mehr als genug.*
MAX. I know you, my carpenter, my cobbler, I know your aphorisms. Naturally the pair of shoes Tolstoy made were a greater achievement than his *War and Peace* and, moreover, you don't have to wear those shoes! Listen, have you thought about the parents?

FRANZ. Yes. Here we go again! There are always parents around, they crawl out of every corner, like mice. Yes, I have thought: when you are probing Jana's parents, I will try to prepare my father. I think I'll do this through mother and only then face to face. But I will await your report.
MAX. You've forgotten a little detail.

(FRANZ looks puzzled)

The young lady, after all, she has to give her consent. Won't it be better if you were first to talk to Jana and then I'll go into the basement as a messenger of love.
FRANZ. No! I'm certain of her agreement. Her face is open towards me, it accepts me, it accepts my looks and thoughts. Her eyes and lips assure me she is agreeable. Have you noticed her splendid teeth, like tiny pearls? She has a certain kind of smile, a little smile meant only for me. We shall come to an understanding without difficulty, without words.
MAX. But eventually she will start talking and she will be talking to you.
FRANZ. Buy her flowers...roses...no! Not roses, buy flowers suitable for the occasion and a large box of chocolates. Make sure it's a large assortment of chocolates with liqueurs and rum.

(MAX and FRANZ walk off stage. Then they re-appear and leave once more. Then MAX re-appears on his own. A girl appears amongst other passers-by. She stops outside the hairdresser's, lights fade.)

TABLEAU VIII

Rings

A large hotel receptions room. Chairs, table, a sofa. The engaged couple with their respective parents. And FELICE'S friend GRETE, all wearing their Sunday best. FELICE has a white lace blouse. She is sitting next to FRANZ'S FATHER with her head inclined towards him. FATHER kisses her hand and FELICE gazes at it.

FATHER. If I were younger...

(FELICE laughs heartily with her mouth wide open showing her teeth with gold crowns)

In this blouse you look like a lily... if I were younger I would abduct you and Franz would be left with his mother!

(FRANZ gazes spellbound at FELICE'S open mouth then wipes his brow with his hand and bows his head)

Lucky devil! He always lands on his four feet.
FELICE. But he is not saying anything.

(Tugs at her handkerchief)

FATHER. He'll speak when he has come to terms with his happiness.

(Gazes at FELICE)

What a pretty blouse! You women are truly bewitching... just a bit of lace, a veil, a scarf, a bracelet and a man's head is turned.
FELICE. Men are like children... they want to be bewitched so we turn ourselves into fairies, but sometimes we have toothache and the spell is broken.

(FELICE again laughs heartily)

FATHER. Dear friends, I am peckish!
FELICE. Men are butterflies so we have to look like flowers... colour, shape, scent, that is what men go for... we lure them, we open up in the sun, we blossom in love's rays.

THE TRAP

FATHER. My child, as an old butterfly I am glad that such a flower as you has come my son's way. But meanwhile Herr Doktor and Insurance Agent lodged in one body appears somewhat strange.
FRANZ. I...
FATHER. For a lawyer our son is not exactly silver-tongued, true, he has opened his mouth twice, but he's only said one word. A short word, but as far as he is concerned the most important word in the world: I.
MOTHER. Hermann... please don't.
FATHER. Dear guests, beloved children, we are gathered here today for an engagement which is a solemn occasion but also a joyful one and full of promise for the future. Though the fiancé behaves as if he was attending a funeral... he opened his mouth twice but got tongue-tied... meanwhile our tummies are rumbling... not quite the sound of a wedding march yet! I'm sure we shall all feel better after some refreshments. A fully-laden table has now been waiting for us this past hour! *"Die Verlobung ihrer Kinder Felice und Franz zeigen ergebenst an!"* And now we shall leave the lovers alone and make our way to the restaurant. Let us proceed!

(All get up ready to move)

FELICE. I won't stay here... I don't even know whether I am engaged!

(MOTHER goes up to FRANZ as if she wished to touch his bowed head but is afraid...)

FATHER. Let's go!
FELICE. I may be a flower but I am hungry...

(About to leave)

FRANZ. Miss Grete...

(GRETE astonished, stops in her tracks. FRANZ mumbling)

Please stay...
GRETE. Felice... did you hear that?
FELICE. This performance has made me feel hungry, I must have a bite.

(Laughs)

Perhaps he'll confess to you.

(Leaves)

FRANZ. *(Gets up, walks silently about the room and sits down on the sofa. Sound of excited voices from the restaurant. FRANZ pulls out a little box, opens it and gazes at the ring).* I have a request to make.

(GRETE remains silent)

Miss Grete, please sit here next to me.

(GRETE stays silent)

Miss Grete, please sit here next to me.

(GRETE stays silent)

Why do you...
GRETE. Herr Doktor, I too feel hungry...
FRANZ. Do you condemn me?
GRETE. What I feel is of no consequence, this is not my engagement. You have a fiancée.
FRANZ. You talk of banalities. What is a fiancée? There are people who spread boredom, nothing but boredom...
GRETE. I can't listen to this. Felice is my friend, this is disgusting.
FRANZ. Why? It's the truth.
GRETE. She has only just left the room.
FRANZ. But I couldn't say all this in front of her! I was terribly bored!
GRETE. *(Smiles, despite herself).* At your own engagement?
FRANZ. Precisely. At Max's engagement I enjoyed myself hugely, I was the spirit of the party, as for my own, it doesn't seem to interest me all that much.
GRETE. Are you making a fool of me? Are you ill? What do you expect from women?
FRANZ. I would like you to sit next to me, I'd like to ask you to help me and Felice. As far as my work is concerned women are a disaster, but in relation to myself alive, or rather dying, they are a salvation. But for my work they are disastrous: they destroy the writing process at its inception, even while it's only a thought in the head...

(GRETE sits on the edge of the sofa and looks carefully at FRANZ)

That's it: silence. You know how to be silent. That's more valuable than the gift of speech. Your silence contains everything, it's most interesting, silence is without doubt a much vaster area than the area of speech and sound. Your words may repel me, but your silence attracts me and draws me. Your silent presence was more valuable than all this chatter which has broken loose over my head. Animals have long periods of silence, trees are silent, the four elements are silent, painting is silent, pictures are dumb...

even music is silent. Beside you I feel innocent, like an animal. Your body speaks to me with its alert immobility, its scent.

(GRETE gets up, FRANZ catches her hand)

Please hold me! Miss Grete! Can't you feel I am drowning? But if you have no human feeling for me at least show a little understanding. Surely a sick dog would make you want to kiss and fondle him. I am not a doctor nor a fiancé, I am a wounded animal, tied up and pushed into this room for slaughter.

GRETE. Aren't you ashamed of yourself?! It was you, it was you who invited us all here, Felice and me, her parents and your mother and father. You've had invitations published in the newspapers! It was you who's drawn us into your beautiful ceremony, and now you are sitting on a sofa with a martyred look and talking a load of rubbish!

FRANZ. And yet you do talk.

GRETE. Can't you understand that what you're doing is ridiculous and quite disgusting?

FRANZ. *(Touches GRETE lightly)*. Your single touch may cure me. Please don't say anything. Foods which nourish us are silent. I have plenty of words but I need nourishment which would turn into my flesh and blood. Words spoil everything. Quite honestly, I don't know why Felice... it's you who are really my fiancée.

GRETE. Herr Doktor, the luncheon party is waiting for us and here you are indulging in this performance!

FRANZ. Please don't go away, please come back to me tomorrow.

GRETE. You are a clown and you make people miserable.

(GRETE gets up)

FRANZ. Miss Grete... please give me your hand...

GRETE. You've selected me as your sacrificial heifer, isn't that so? You will stun me, drag me to your lair and eat me raw... or place me on the altar of literature. The only thing is that I am not suitable for sacrifice, you have been led astray by my appearance. I would tame and train you so you would be eating out of this hand for the rest of your life, like a circus dog or pony. You should eat everything without protests and lamentations. You, Herr Doktor, have to be kept at close rein, held by the snout!

FRANZ. *(Thoughtfully looks at GRETE's hand without listening to her words)*. You have a paw like... for a moment I thought you had six little fingers... but I made a mistake... pity, that sixth utterly useless little finger would have been my choice... I would have placed my engagement ring upon it... now please go in there and announce to the assembly that I regard my engagement to Felice as broken off. As for the ring...

TABLEAU VIII

(He slips the ring on GRETE's finger)

GRETE. You make a mockery of people! It was you who invited us all to your engagement. Nobody but you.
FRANZ. I have a migraine...I couldn't eat a thing without vomiting.
GRETE. You're simply afraid...can't you understand I am her friend? After all, you are a writer.

(Tries to remove the ring)

FRANZ. I don't know...I have an axe stuck in my head...I can't eat lunch with an axe in my skull. Can't you see I am bleeding, that blood and sweat are pouring down my body?
GRETE. I don't understand similes and allegories. You're simply afraid like a little boy who has wet his pants! You're afraid of daddy, of mummy, of Felice and, of course, you are using me to wipe you, to change your pants and sing you to sleep. That's a prank one may expect from a little boy, but not from an insurance agent and doctor of law. He appears to be dying and drags a woman into bed! Are you going to join them or not?!

(FRANZ arranges himself on the sofa, his hands on his chest. He remains silent. GRETE pulls the ring off her finger and throws it down. She glances at FRANZ, clenches her fist, shakes it at him and runs out.)

TABLEAU IX

The harbinger

The cobbler's workshop in the basement. The white curtain in the window is pulled back. Through the window, men's and women's legs and boots. Occasionally the bare feet of a running child. The COBBLER sitting on a stool at his bench repairing shoes. Next to him on the floor a dishevelled boy of seven is polishing a variety of men's and women's shoes and boots. Occasionally he stops and stares into space and then starts polishing again with redoubled energy. A curtain or screen divides the room, and behind the screen the kitchen where the COBBLER'S WIFE is busy. There is a clatter of dishwashing, children's chatter, laughter, a baby crying and a cradle rocking. The parade of legs through the window continues throughout, though the rhythm of the movement varies. A bell rings and MAX enters the workshop down a staircase. He is clutching a colossal bunch of carnations in one hand, and in the other, a large box of chocolates tied with a red ribbon, and an umbrella. He is wearing a bowler, a coat, light-coloured gloves and patent leather shoes. Speaks grandiloquently in the belief that the news he is about to announce to this family requires a framework. But since the young lady's family is not aware of what is imminent, it behaves normally and courteously. From time to time someone pulls back the screen which divides the workshop from the kitchen and children's heads can be seen. It all looks like an amateur theatre just before a performance. Subdued whispers and giggles emerge from behind the curtain. Throughout the scene the children appear and disappear from behind the screen. The COBBLER'S WIFE's sweaty face also appears for a moment.

COBBLER. (*Stops hammering, nods, holds a mouthful of nails so his speech is indistinct*). Good morning, Herr Professor ... Zenek fetch Herr Professor a seat.

(*The boy stops polishing shoes and hands MAX a stool, he spits on it and polishes it with his sleeve. MAX glances at the stool, but remains standing. Now the COBBLER's WIFE appears through the screen with a chair which she polishes with a cloth.*)

COBBLER'S WIFE. Excuse me, sit down, have no fear!

(*She disappears behind the screen*)

MAX. (*Still standing*). Thank you, madam, please do not disturb yourself, it makes no difference to me, I am quite happy sitting on a stool. Please don't stop for me, I know too well how much a lady of the house, a wife and a mother has to cope with in a day.

(Approaches the stool but ZENEK pushes the chair towards him, then stops in front of MAX watching him. He is still holding the flowers, the umbrella and the chocolates. He now rests the flowers and chocolates on his knees, takes off his bowler, feels hot in his coat. Puts on his bowler, unbuttons his coat, takes off his glasses and polishes them: he fidgets all the time.)

COBBLER. Zenek! The Herr Professor's shoes, at once!
MAX. Let's drop these official titles, my friend. I am here today in a private capacity.
COBBLER. I am sure the Herr Professor is on his way to a party, judging by the things for the ladies. Zenek, pack the... Zenek, stop staring at the Herr Professor... pack those shoes in a newspaper immediately... would you like Zenek to order a cab? Better for the flowers and parcels.
MAX. *(Placing on the floor some of the various objects he is holding)*. In a sense these flowers are intended by my friend for Miss Jana, but in case she is not present, I will take the liberty of presenting the flowers to your respected wife, should she allow me, my dear Herr Joseph! Young man! Please present the flowers to your mummy so that she may place them in a vase of water.

(Hands the flowers to ZENEK who continues staring at MAX. The COBBLER now stops his work and turns fully towards his guest. Meanwhile MAX pats ZENEK on the head and pushes him behind the screen. In a moment there is a sound of pots and pans being pushed aside and the indistinct voices of the COBBLER'S WIFE and her children. MAX places the chocolates on the stool and his bowler on top of the chocolates and, looking at the COBBLER, slowly takes off his gloves and wipes his glasses with an handkerchief. The COBBLER wipes his hands on his apron. A little girl comes up to the stool, touches the chocolates with her finger and then withdraws it rapidly.)

The matter which has caused me, or rather caused my friend, whom I represent at this moment... is of an exceptionally delicate nature. There are certain intimate spheres of personal and emotional life in which my friend does not feel at all comfortable. His psyche does not permit him a direct confrontation with reality. This is not, God forbid, any lack of courage: despite the fact that in his professional work he comes across the most prosaic aspects of life, nevertheless he frequently is unable to understand the simplest things. He sees, let us say, a girl, a maiden, and thinks that that person is... this is difficult to express... he is simply surprised to learn that that maiden has a father, a mother, perhaps a brother or a sister, never mind an aunt or a grandfather. He is equally surprised by husbands. In a word, my friend, who penetrates everything in the sphere of the spirit, is,

TABLEAU IX

as far as human relations are concerned, a child. He thinks that the lady of his choice has emerged from Jove's head or from sea spray. My friend reacts totally unexpectedly to various stimuli. For instance, he will construct his future nest in pedantic detail, but should he catch a whiff of boiled cauliflower in his fiancée's house, he runs away in panic and the whole structure falls apart.

(From behind the screen, a girl enters the workshop carrying a broom and a mug. She takes a large sip, then blows the water all over the floor and begins to sweep it. She is looking at MAX and sweeps all around him.)

COBBLER. We seem to be speaking the same language, and yet I can't see what the Herr Professor is getting at in this case...I think, with the Herr Professor's permission, the old woman is boiling cabbage not cauliflower.

MAX. My dear Herr Joseph, let's leave aside cabbage and cauliflower, and let us go back to the matter which has brought me here! Once more I have to stress that my friend possesses civil courage to a greater degree than the average citizen, but this courage does not extend to the sphere of family life or relationships with the gentle sex. In a word, he thinks a girl ripens like a fruit on a tree without the help of parents, without brothers and sisters, cousins or relatives. In a word, my friend faces an ordinary uncle or brother-in-law like something unexpected and even somewhat terrifying. He takes various phenomena for granted and yet a brother-in-law amazes him! I remember we had quite an unpleasant scene on account of my brother-in-law. He happened to be staying with us and when I introduced him to Franz, instead of introducing himself or shaking his hand, Franz kept staring at him in silence, or rather kept examining him in a highly improper manner, until at a certain moment he began to repeat, as if in complete amazement, the word "brother-in-law" stressing different syllables each time, and then he began to laugh! My brother-in-law was furious and left the room while Franz, looking at me, said sadly, "So my friend, you have a brother-in-law..."

(During this speech MAX gets carried away, he ends it suddenly with a squeak and begins to wipe his face with a handkerchief. He keeps buttoning and unbuttoning his coat, polishing his glasses, he rubs his hands and folds and unfolds his arms on his chest.)

COBBLER. Herr Professor, please take your coat off and feel quite at home. Zenek! Take the Herr Professor's coat! I hope you feel better now. Would you like some water?

COBBLER'S WIFE. *(Appears from behind the screen clutching a vase full of carnations).* Thank you for the flowers and my profound apologies for this mess!

MAX. *(Sits down, gets up).* Madam, my dear sir, I have the honour, in the name of my friend, a clerk with a suitable position and a suitable dwelling, with university education, to ask you, as Miss Jana's parents, to allow him to pay you an official visit, should my mission also find favour with your daughter.

(The COBBLER gets up and bows. Behind the curtain children's voices, screams and giggles: a voice calling out a rhyme accompanying a game and a red-haired little girl with a wreath on her head is pushed out in front of the screen. The girl watches MAX solemnly.)

COBBLER'S WIFE. Please forgive us.

(She disappears behind the curtain with the flowers)

COBBLER. I can't make head or tail of this. Zenek, run along to Mr. Hasek and bring us three beers. No wait, take the empties and bring five.

(ZENEK collects the empties into a bag)

Tell Mr. Hasek I'll pay him personally. If I got it right, it's to do with our Jana who won't be back from work until the evening, but tell me, please, why hasn't this gentleman come along personally to ask for her hand?

MAX. There is a hallowed custom for such declarations and even for engagements to be performed "per procura".

COBBLER. Zenek! Get lost! This conversation is not for children. Beat it! You will agree, sir, it's better not to talk in front of the children—soon the whole neighbourhood will be talking about this.

(MAX gets up, the COBBLER sits down)

"Per procura!" But you can't make a pair of shoes without the client's foot! And if he has his own length of leather, he still has to come personally to get measured up. He may be educated but, if you pardon the expression, he has feet like anybody else.

(The COBBLER presses against MAX and speaks with passion)

You need God's gift in everything, that's why there are now so many artists, and so few good cobblers.

COBBLER'S WIFE. *(Peeps out for a moment and speaks from behind the screen).* Herr Professor, please don't listen to his ramblings. He drinks beer all day and gets his tongue in a twist! Would you like some tea? Pull yourself together! Aren't you ashamed in front of the children?!

MAX. But I was listening to Herr Joseph with the utmost pleasure.

(Pulls on his gloves)

TABLEAU IX

COBBLER. Herr Professor, I don't know what your religion is but I think only the old-fashioned orthodox Jews can speak Czech so beautifully and accurately.
MAX. *(Patting the COBBLER on the shoulder)*. My friend, please remember, that when we are silent we are one, but when we begin to speak we are two. An old Zen proverb.
COBBLER'S WIFE. *(From the kitchen)*. There, see, smart boots, the Professor has shut you up. Please be seated Herr Professor. We'll both sit down and you'll put your cards on the table. Take the Professor's coat.

(MAX takes off his coat, gloves and scarf and hands them to the COBBLER who holds the things looking at MAX)

Tell the mother everything "procura" and you may be assured, Herr Professor, that a mother's heart understands everything.
COBBLER. *(Shaking his head)*. Say what you like, but things must follow in the proper order. If you want her, take her, but things must take their proper turn, that's for sure: first the engagement, then the wedding and only then: bang! Whether he is procuring or not procuring, the young man must behave himself. Zenek! Run to Mr. Hasek and fetch another five bottles of Pilz—but at once!

(Behind the screen, there are now squeals and giggles as if all the children were playing hide and seek. Through the basement window we can see the feet and boots of marching soldiers and there is the sound of a lively march. All the characters are now drawn towards the window and watch fascinated: the march can be heard for quite a while and flowers can be seen falling among the marching feet.)

TABLEAU X

Brothers and Sisters

A black wall at the back of the stage. A green lawn. FRANZ is sleeping under an apple tree. He is wearing a black waistcoat and a white shirt with rolled up-sleeves. OTTLA enters wearing a simple country dress and a head scarf. She stops next to FRANZ, bends over and looks at his face. The sisters ELLI and VALLI run into the garden wearing colourful summer dresses. They hold hands and dance. OTTLA presses her fingers to her lips. The sisters bend over FRANZ and sing.

ELLI and VALLI. *Schlaf, Herzli, schlaf,*
schlaf, mein kleiner Graf,
bis der Hahn am Morgen fruh
lustig ruf sein Guggenu!
Schlafe, schlafe sieben Stund,
bis der Vater wieder kummt.

OTTLA. Franz has been working all morning. He has brought handsaws to cut the branches, pruning shears, spades and a hammer. And also a whole boxful of manuals: *Establishing a Fruit Garden, Fruit Gardens and the Climate, Rejuvenating Trees, Storing Fruit.* He reads through the night. Yesterday at dinner he gave us a lecture on mineral and natural fertilizers. He told me to set up a compost heap on my farm. He criticized us for burning potato stems in the autumn instead of using them as compost, since when they decay they produce compost which is an excellent substitute for cow dung. But he displayed most enthusiasm when we had pudding. He even raised his index finger and delivered a sermon "ex cathedra".

(OTTLA raises her index finger and mimics FRANZ's lecture on manures)

"Faeces are an inadequately exploited source of mineral and organic elements. It is not possible to use faeces in vegetable patches for health reasons, but there can be no objection against them in fruit gardens. They can be distributed directly from the container into furrows dug below the trees, but outside the perimeters of their crowns, and then covered up with earth.

(ELLI and VALLI are eating apples)

Faeces are a very concentrated and powerfully active manure and, therefore, their transportation from the city into the fruit gardens is a rewarding investment! This long lecture on the subject of faeces and the irresposibility of city dwellers who waste a valuable organic product ended with a parable about the variety of views one might have regarding, for instance, an apple: "The viewpoint of the little boy who had to stretch his neck in order to see the apple on the table and the viewpoint of the mistress of the house who takes the apple and with an easy gesture passes it on to a guest."

(ELLI and VALLI run round the garden laughing and bickering while OTTLA is sorting out the fruit. EXECUTIONER-GUARDS appear against the black wall at the back of the stage. They wear black uniforms and are handling a police dog on a leash. They pass quickly against the wall and then a dog barking can be heard — they were not noticed: VALLI and ELLI whisper to each other and laugh. OTTLA is trimming branches with her secateurs. FRANZ wakes up, listens, dogs are barking in the distance. The EXECUTIONERS' activities are unpredictable. They may return on the stage at any moment with or without their dogs. They may enter the dining room during a meal, a bedroom at night, they may enter the garden ... they may enter in silence and may stop in front of selected people. The EXECUTIONERS' activities are unpredictable. Sometimes the characters notice them, sometimes only one character does while the others behave as though they weren't there. FRANZ looks at OTTLA)

OTTLA. You are all in a sweat...

(Stroking him)

FRANZ. I'm hungry... what's for dinner?
OTTLA. Spinat mit Setzei und Kartoffeln...
FRANZ. Ausgezeichnet!
OTTLA. Mit guter Butter gemacht!
FRANZ. Ausgezeichnet! Gemüseschitzel, dann Nudeln mit Apfelmus — Ausgezeichnet!
OTTLA. Tomatensalat, Semmel, Pflaumenkompott.
FRANZ, VALLI and ELLI. (In unison). Ausgezeichnet!!

(ELLI and VALLI leave. OTTLA sits down next to FRANZ while he rests his head on her knees, staring at her face and eyes and the sky beyond.)

FRANZ. I push away sleep, I'm afraid I'll sleep my life away, and here at your place in the country I would like to be alert day and night. I worry I'll sleep through and miss everything that's most beautiful: the shade under the apple tree, the light on your face, the cock crowing. I'm afraid I'll fall asleep and someone will steal all these things from me and I'll wake up in a locked chest or wardrobe smelling of mouse droppings and dead animals.
OTTLA. You can't forget.

TABLEAU X

FRANZ. I can't even tell now if it was a drean or just a thought. Maybe it was a story I hadn't written and that's why it's torturing me, biting me, trying to eat its way through my skin and become a reality. There was some enormous wardrobe or a linen cupboard with a drawer at the bottom. I was alone in the darkness. The room had lost its walls and its ceiling, as happens at night. I heard squeals, shuffling and rustling, I thought it's probably the mice eating up my papers, my letters, my stories. I was nauseated at the thought of opening the drawer and suddenly there was silence inside. I began opening it slowly, until I could see inside, and there was this crowd, this mass, this stinking black whirling bustle, but these weren't mice, these were people, a human ant-heap. They were wearing overalls like Jews from the east. I felt nausea, and pushed the drawer back, then I started opening it. It seemed they were short of air, they had no food because they were pushing towards the opening, squealing and grunting, but suddenly I felt a cruelty that you get in quiet, well-behaved children.

OTTLA. Even in your dreams you torture yourself, and others. Sometimes I would like to enter your head, enter your brain and get everything sorted out: to wipe away the ghosts and vampires that make you so miserable. When I hold you in my arms, I am your shield. I love you very much. I would like you to know that.

FRANZ. In there, they were suffering and squealing and I kept opening and shutting the drawer, watching with disgust their tiny, hairy paws, their pink snouts, their rolling eyes, their beards and side-curls. They disgusted me like those flies on the fly-paper that Josie used to throw into the fire where they sizzled and crackled. Only one individual escaped from this swarm because I didn't shut the door in time, he was too quick for me. He was standing there before me, now appearing like a little boy who, unlike the overalled crowd, was wearing a tight-fitting, buttoned-up jacket. It was Max, I recognised him. He kept buttoning up and unbuttoning that coat, checking the buttons, his lips salivating and with a devilishly malicious little smile he was full of that passion for lecturing everyone. His hand stretched towards me, his index finger aimed at my breast, he keeps asking me something. His voice is sharp and he has instant arguments to prove everything. Now his voice is like that of a canary, this tiny voice drilling into my ears, into my head. Now he is squealing as if he were presenting me with an ultimatum, yes or no. I understand what he means and I am filled with unspeakable terror which you feel only in moments of agony.

OTTLA. It's all because you shut yourself up. You shut yourself up, you slam the door on the world, you lock it out and you build a trap, a burrow, with tremendous effort and the sweat of your brow; and you fall into it ill and tormented. All you have to do is open the door. Life begins outside, you take your first step, then the next, and away you fly!

FRANZ. I am a trap, my body is a trap that caught me after birth.

OTTLA. I, too, used to be afraid of what's lurking behind the door against which someone's enormous body is pressing. The door opened. It was father who had barred the door and he renounced me and I left everyone behind me. I flew out, and beyond the door was the country, fields, orchards, gardens, beehives; there were meadows and the smell of hay. I was running away and only your eyes were accompanying me, they were pushing me towards the light and life, and now you're here with me and you can stay here till the end as my guardian and my child.

FRANZ. I do sometimes think of escaping, maybe I'll free myself at last. I'll write for a living, I'll go somewhere abroad, to Palestine maybe, or Russia. Russia! Its magnetic power is infinite. I'll get off the train somewhere beyond Tula and I'll march ahead. A colossal, unimaginable river with yellow waves...Felice is deaf to all my requests which I present to her in sign language. She yearns for the happiness of the average, for a comfortable apartment, a bedroom, heated rooms and well stocked wardrobes, linen cupboards and dressers. She even expects me to take an interest in her father's factory and she likes to eat well. She eats meat, even though meat gets between your teeth! Only wild animals have teeth adapted to tearing and chewing meat! Like all her friends she wants to sleep until 11:00—and at night? I don't know. She sets my watch which has been an hour ahead for a year now and gets it absolutely right. She doesn't understand my rhythm, my time in which a clock may be an hour ahead because this rhythm has no meaning for my basic and only important activity which is writing.

OTTLA. Are you afraid of this marriage? If you are, I'll tell her.

FRANZ. She has a mouth full of gold teeth! I'll tell you in confidence—when I first knew her I used to shut my eyes in shame and fear when Felice laughed showing all her teeth and palate!

OTTLA. You're a fool!

FRANZ. It's all in her mouth!

OTTLA. My dear brother! And where do you expect a girl to have her teeth?

FRANZ. A hellish abyss full of shining teeth! But healthy gums full of teeth are also terrible and in fact it was thanks to this handicap that Felice appeared to me more precious. It was a small defect which couldn't be disguised and therefore inspires a feeling of...it's difficult to describe...something like tenderness...although as a fiance I might have objected to gold teeth and yet I have never done so to her...you know...people don't seem to bother about their teeth.

OTTLA. Mummy is terribly upset about the broken engagement. People do care about formalities. You've placed advertisements again, you've asked her parents and then you say you have a headache and break off the engagement, or rather you don't say anything. I am, and I shall always be, with you and on your side but mummy reasons like an ordinary woman...and as for father?!

FRANZ. It's blood...blood from inside my organism has flowed out and broken off the engagement. My organism gave me to understand that I am to do only one thing: write. Marriages, pregnancies and buying wardrobes had to be left to the chosen, to the lucky ones. But the teeth—would you believe it that last week I had a letter from a certain girl who complained that her teeth ache and says that this is due to draughts. How can a grown-up write such nonsense! It's healthy teeth that feel best when exposed to streams of air and despite the respect due to a young lady I asked her point blank about her dental hygiene and whether she brushes them after every meal.

OTTLA. *(Shaking her head).* No, no, Franz, do please put yourself in the position of your fiancée and her parents.

FRANZ. *Liebes Fräulein Grete,* I say to her...

OTTLA. Grete?! That friend of Felice's?

FRANZ. Maybe you do brush your teeth thoroughly, but do believe me it's meat which is the prime cause of tooth decay. I know from my own experience: there you are sitting at table, laughing, entertaining them with conversation and meanwhile the bits of meat stuck between your teeth cause infection in the mouth cavity. The meat rots, we could say in front of our eyes, the bacteria and infection arising from the rotting remnants and gristle of the meat, as it might be from a dead rat squashed between a couple of stones.

OTTLA. But what has Grete to do with this?!

FRANZ. It was Grete who told me a lot about the frequent toothache that Felice suffers. And you must know, dear sister, that of all diseases it is toothache that frightens and disgusts me most. True, cleaning teeth at table is not pleasant for others, still one should remove strands of meat at once. Remember, only father had the unwritten right to pick his teeth at table. He used to pick them with a toothpick and at times used his fork or his fingernail. He would also crush the bones, suck out the marrow, smack his lips and pull out strands of meat stuck between his teeth and at the same time yell at us for poking about our mouths at table.

OTTLA. *(Smiling).* So it's to do with picking your teeth...

FRANZ. Carnivourous animals have spiky, widely spaced teeth adapted to tearing and crushing meat, while people...

OTTLA. While people have sent you presents! Uncle Alfred in Madrid has written a beautiful letter with a cheque for 1000 crowns, as a wedding present for Felice and you. What happened to that cheque?! Mother will have to send it back and explain to Uncle Alfred...

FRANZ. Felice spent all her time talking about furnishing the apartment, even though I made it quite clear that when I'm married I still must have somewhere to work. My burrow, like a rat's or a badger's. You don't entertain guests in a burrow. A guest who peers into a burrow or pushes in univited turns into our enemy. From me Felice demands feelings which she doesn't bestow on my sisters. She calls Valli an ironing board and Elli a goose. And she hasn't even noticed you. As far as she is concerned you're some useless comic creation rather than my youngest sister. She ought to know you are my only ally in the battle. I suspect she hasn't read in full a single story of mine even though she reads Austrian and other novels. I am not jealous, once I gave her *The Kreutzer Sonata* and I am sure she hasn't read it.

OTTLA. *The Kreutzer Sonata* is not encouraging reading for a future wife and mother. Tolstoy's wife wasn't impressed with the book either, she felt deeply wounded. As for your letters to Grete...

FRANZ. *(Aside)*. Am I afraid of marriage? Perhaps, perhaps I am afraid: in marriage you have children: children who may pay us back with a little extra all our sins against our own parents. If I were to stand facing my own son and he were so dried up, self-absorbed and silent, in a word, what if I were to have a son resembling me?! Most likely I would run away from him, walk out, just as our own father thought of doing.

(One of the EXECUTIONER-GUARDS enters and points to OTTLA. FRANZ is arranging apples in a basket and doesn't notice him. OTTLA, incredulous, puts her hand to her breast as if she meant to ask "Is it me, is this to do with me?" The EXECUTIONER nods. OTTLA brushes down her blouse and skirt and follows the EXECUTIONER on tip-toe. They walk along the black wall and disappear in the darkness. FRANZ doesn't notice what is going on behind his back along the black wall. A distant baying of hounds.) (A man appears against the black wall, holding a book. He opens it and reads)

MAN with BOOK. On the way leading from the gas chamber to the graves, that is the space of a few hundred metres, stood a group of dentists with pliers. They would open the corpse's mouth, inspect it and remove gold teeth and gold crowns which they threw into a basket. There were eight dentists. On they whole they were young people detained from the transports to perform these duties. One of them I knew quite well, his name was Zucker. He came from Rzeszów. The dentists were housed in a separate hut. In the evening they would bring basketfuls of gold teeth into the hut where they would separate the gold and turn it into slabs. They were guarded by a Gestapo man who beat them if they didn't work fast enough. The bars were 1cm. thick, ½ cm. wide and 20 cm. long.

(Now in silence EXECUTIONER-GUARDS steer a herd of naked people turned into cattle, led to slaughter along the black wall. FRANZ neither sees nor hears, wholly engrossed in inspecting the trees, their leaves, branches and fruit. Three female shapes break off from the crowd. They are OTTLA, VALLI and ELLI. They are naked and shield their nakedness with their hands and hair. Someone throws old rags and shoes in their direction. OTTLA collects a man's shirt, torn pants, ragged trousers and a Russian prisoner's shirt: on her head a headscarf and on her arm a white band with the Star of David. She is wearing sandals. ELLI and VALLI are still searching for clothes. OTTLA comes up to her brother from behind and puts her palms over his eyes. FRANZ laughs.)

TABLEAU X

OTTLA. *Eins zwei drei,*
du bist frei,
FRANZ. *Vier funf sechs,*
du bist nex
OTTLA. *(Takes off her headscarf and ties it around FRANZ'S eyes and then turns him round several times)*
Eichen, Buchen, Tannen,
und du musst fangen.
Eichen, Tannen, Buchen,
und du musst suchen!

(ELLI and VALLI are searching for food by the wall. One has found a bone, the other a few potatoes and they move fearfully towards the edge of the garden but do not cross into it. They are dressed in dirty rags and are tearing at their finds. On their backs and across their breasts they have the Star of David or the inscription "Jude". FRANZ runs around with his eyes tied up. ELLI, VALLI and OTTLA run along the black wall. They disappear in the darkness.)

(Now the garden is silent. FRANZ runs about for a little while and then tears off the band. He looks around smiling, places his palms against his lips and cries.)

FRANZ. Elli, Valli, Ottla, Elli, Valli, Ottla!

(An echo in the depths responds, multiplying the sounds and then dies away. Slowly a cold dead light fills the stage, killing all colour, everything turns into smoke and ashes.)

TABLEAU XI

I'll stoke the fire with my friend's hands

A large room with trees through the window. An ornamental tiled stove, its open door showing a fire glowing inside. Light through the window slowly fades. FRANZ is walking about the room, stopping from time to time to warm his hands. The leaping red flame surrounds his black silhouette. FRANZ picks up a poker and pokes the fire. On a table near the stove there are papers, notebooks and newspapers. The tree beyond the window grows dark. FRANZ is talking to himself. At first he mumbles intermittently, repeats certain words and at last a coherent speech emerges.

FRANZ. Dort unten in der Mühle,
Sass ich in süsser Ruh,
Und sah dem Räderspiele
Und sah den Wassern zu,
Sah zu der blanken Säge.
Es war mir wie ein Traum,
Die bahnte lange Wege
In einen Tannenbaum,
Die Tanne war wie lebend
In Trauermelodie.

(*FRANZ pours himself a glass of red wine, examines it against the light and drinks it slowly. MAX comes in and they embrace.*)

MAX. Here I am.

(*FRANZ steps backwards and looks at MAX*)

What's the matter?! I received your telegram yesterday evening. I travelled all night.
FRANZ. Nothing has happened. Nothing really.

(*He lights a lamp*)

As you see I am going through my papers.
MAX. Papers?

FRANZ. I am burning papers and letters.

MAX. You are burning other people's letters, while your letters...!

FRANZ. I am also burning my works, I am saying goodbye to them and throwing them into the fire. The tray is now full of ash. These aren't "papers," these are live beings, I can hear their cries and screams, these are my aborted children which I had impregnated within myself. My seed gushed inwards but I have overestimated my powers, Max. I can't burn my own children, only you can do this.

MAX. You're ill. This is delirious talk.

FRANZ. With your hands I want you to burn everything I have given birth to... After my death...

MAX. You have invented this torture to punish me for the friendship you have shown me... you hate me, you can't forgive anyone close to you for being a writer. You grow wild when somebody tells you he is a writer too. You laugh hysterically! Isn't it true that you want to punish me even after your death for my being a writer because I love your work which you despise? Why wait? Let's burn everything now, working together, then we'll drink a glass of wine and it'll all be over!

FRANZ. You see, I'm no longer able to burn them, they plead for a stay of execution. Shut up in drawers and lacking air they suffocate, but they want to live. It'll be easier for you, even though, as you say, you love them more than your own. Burning manuscripts and books is neither as cruel nor as stupid as people generally make out. Books have been, and always will be destroyed by various churches, institutions, ideologies. They have been, and they will be destroyed, by writers who have seen through them and are in despair. I don't want them to live in this world persecuted by censors, spat at by idiots, tamed by commentators. Some I have already burnt, and those in the suitcase are meant for you, you'll burn them on the day I am buried.

MAX. *(Looks at the suitcase against the wall).* I want to put a question to you... I've been meaning to put this question to you for years, but I haven't had the courage.

FRANZ. *(Laughing).* So now the hidden dagger!

MAX. I am sorry but this dagger is as soft as your friend's hand.

FRANZ. A damp, soft hand.

MAX. *(Pointing his index-finger with his arm outstretched towards FRANZ's chest).* Why is it that whenever you have to face life you make use of other people?

(FRANZ moves over towards the stove and stands in silence with his back to MAX)

Apart from writing and dying you've always wanted to so things by proxy, using Ottla, your mother, several other women and the faithful Max... can you answer this question?

FRANZ. *(Still with his back to MAX).* First of all relax, have a wash. As you can see I live in comfort, even luxury. I have a bath, though the tiles remind me of scrambled eggs.

TABLEAU XI

MAX. *(Picking up the suitcase)*. It's heavy! I've had a wash in the train, thank you. You called me, so I rushed over, I'm here, but now you have to answer.

FRANZ. I love you, surely you know this, though from the time you got married my feelings have been tainted with a touch of pity and disgust. Don't be angry.

MAX. There you are, rat, burrowing again! Again you want to hide but you must answer the question.

FRANZ. This isn't a question, this is a noose.

MAX. Please reply.

FRANZ. I don't understand you.

MAX. I'll jog your memory, then. It all started at school, I caught your attentive glance, I felt you wanted to know me but you kept asking other boys about me even though I was near you and could hear your voice. In the Fourth Form we had a ginger-haired boy from the country and you chose him as a go-between. He came to me with the message that you were congratulating me on my essay on Kerner's poem *Der Wanderer in der Sägemühle*.

FRANZ. *Du kehrst zu rechten Stunde*
    O Wanderer, hierein,
    Du bists, für den wie Wunde
    Mir dringst ins Herz hinein!

MAX. *Du bists, für den wir werden*
    Wenn kurz gewandert du,
    Dies Holz im Schoss der Erden
    Ein Schrein zur langen Ruh!

FRANZ. *Vier Bretter sah ich fallen,*
    Mir ward's ums Herze schwer...

(FRANZ walks over to the table and pours out two glasses of wine)

MAX. Ginger came over to me at break... I remember his eyes like forget-me-nots.

FRANZ. *(Picks up his glass). Vergissmeinnicht!*

MAX. *(Clinking glasses with FRANZ)*. He looks at me and says solemnly that you've asked him to congratulate me on my splendid essay! This was so extraordinary and comical between two boys, and in the same class at that, that I began to laugh. I laughed long and loud, and even struck the bench with my fist. The messenger waited patiently for my reply while you sat in a corner taking no notice. I thought of going over to you but you started to write something. You were probably pretending to be busy, so I didn't move. That was our first conversation. And then it was I who became your deputy and go-between.

(MAX drinks up his wine)

When they started dance-lessons at school with pupils from the girls' grammar school you didn't turn up at the first lesson. You informed me you had a temperature, that you had to stay in bed and I should see you immediately after the lesson. Lying in bed you questioned me closely about the progress of the lesson; you asked me to show you the basic steps and figures of ballroom dancing, and as I was an awful dancer you laughed until you cried! Instead of girl partners we had to make do with classmates or chairs. I had to demonstrate how Helmut danced with a chair and Peter danced with Charles and then you often danced with a chair.

FRANZ. *(Quietly).* That's all over, it's gushed out of my lungs on a wave of blood.

MAX. Now you want to use my hands to burn your manuscripts, but I want to know why you are using me...why me....No...that which is your life...why should I murder your offspring? You could have used your cleaning lady who dusts around you and stokes the stove. She must always be searching for paper to light fires. You could have given her these papers—I know why you didn't, shall I tell you?

(FRANZ pokes the fire)

Because that woman can't read! That's why. She can't read!

(MAX's face is now close to FRANZ'S)

But I can read and write and that's why you have chosen me.

FRANZ. I have chosen you because I love you and trust you to execute my last will.

MAX. You've chosen me because you wish to punish me for being a writer too.

FRANZ. You're upset; in the light of these leaping flames this whole business does acquire a hellish look. We need a different light.

(FRANZ switches on the lights)

You give simple matters a sinister twist. I just no longer have the resistance. I begin to read, then lose myself. I have chosen you as the only witness and the last reader. After my death you'll read these manuscripts and then you'll burn them all.

MAX. If I am to burn them, why should I read them! This doesn't make sense.

FRANZ. *(Like someone caught red-handed).* Well...yes...you're probably right...you needn't read them but you must burn them. Let's shake on this agreement. Give me your word.

(MAX stretches out his hand to FRANZ but FRANZ doesn't see it or pretends he doesn't see it and keeps poking the fire)

Thank you...why don't you sit down and tell me how things are, how things are at home, or rather in my father's home. Max, I have some excel-

TABLEAU XI

lent cheese... have you seen my mother and father? They wrote to me saying they'll be visiting me. This visit isn't convenient for me, there's no reason for it, you see. In any case, when you can give them a detailed account of our meeting, about how I live, what I eat and drink... I'm not that ill... or perhaps I shall go to Prague... I eat fruit and nuts, I drink milk and beer... in other words they won't see and hear more from me than from you.

MAX. I did see your mother and Ottla; your father wasn't at home... or perhaps he was.

FRANZ. *(Laughs — picks out hazelnuts from a basket, cracks them with a nutcracker and hands them to MAX).* Do you remember the words he once uttered, all those years ago? "I carry him inside me, I carry him whole!"

MAX. He is your father.

FRANZ. You are wrong! He is not only my father, he is also your father, he is the father we share. He is the father of a million young men who are now fighting and dying; he is the one common father who sends his sons to slaughter, if only by the very fact of giving them life in our putrid world. He is the father who speaks in the voice of God the Father; *Die Leibe kann nur durch Opfer und Schlachtung des Sohnes erreicht werden!* My father's voice carries well. Perhaps he was deliberately talking so loudly so that we should hear his words in the hall. He was talking to mother but he was branding those words on your skin, on your forehead: "Why should Franz choose that chicken-arsed ninny for a friend! His damp warm hands feel like a sponge! And those piercing little eyes, those wire spectacles, drooping on that spotted arse-face! Makes you sick!" We stood there frozen, staring at each other, and because mother tried to calm him down he spoke even louder! "I'm quite sure that squirt masturbates in every dark corner; have you seen his rat-like teeth, that smile of his? I felt like grabbing him by the collar and carrying him downstairs." Without doing up your coat you ran out of the house in a mad flight, and I followed you, miserable and hating father.

MAX. *(Buttons and unbuttons his coat, takes off his glasses which he polishes with his handkerchief. His mouth twisted into a grimace as though he were about to cry or laugh).* You remember every word...

FRANZ. It's me he'd insulted, not you... as far as you were concerned he was just a vulgar boor, a money-maker, but for me he was the father who begat me. Well, it's all past and gone. You are now a brilliant columnist, a respected writer, a husband, head of a family; and I am a doctor of law, a secretary, the author of books.

(MAX picks up a banana from the table and starts peeling it)

You can deceive women; a mother, sister, grandmother. In fact they know nothing of the sexual life of a six-year-old boy, of a teenager, of a youth, of a man and of an old man. They know nothing of our hidden fire and our hidden agonies. Women worry when we look pale, when we have rings under our eyes, or are not eating well. They are astounded by our outbursts of wild fury and our suicides, but fathers and older brothers know everything, while the younger ones guess, snoop, and remain silently terrified. If these women could see us in a cage as we circle, as we knock against the bars and walls, as we moan and stifle the male's cry when separated from the female! Ah well, perhaps it's better they don't see us, that they close their eyes when they copulate with us, that they don't see the faces of newborn rapists, vandals and executioners. And then we weep like a child at a woman's breast.

MAX. *(Continues eating and then carefully wipes his hands on his handkerchief)*. There are different natures, some roar, some get bored ...

FRANZ. Yes, there are different natures, my father knew that well when he tried to take me to a brothel. I never forgave him for that, although he was right and I was a coward; men know everything about each other. Do you remember Tolstoy's *The Death of Ivan Ilyitch*? The son would arouse his father's emotions: "He was terrified by his furtive look" as he read on his son's face that shameful sign with which nature brands small wankers. And this is what father read in our faces: we were boys overfed on meat and all the other goodies which damage teeth and the digestion. We were lazy, sensual, hating sport and physical toil. Such children are always self-absorbed. I was like that and so were you. Father knew it and we disgusted him. You seemed to him weak and abomidable. He never disguised his opinions. He always hit right between the eyes. I was already thirty when he cried out to me, "Wie lange hast du gezögert, ehe du reif geworden bist?!" This applies both to me and to you. Even though you've set up a family, have normal marital relations with your wife, and will become a father while I am on my way to the next world, even though we have matured together, you to life and I to death, we still are in fear of my father as we were twenty years ago. In his presence we are school boys with sweaty palms and feet.

MAX. *(Shrugs his shoulders and picks up an apple from the plate)*. Your father never understood you, he was interested in the works, in the shop, in food, in his own health and that of his family, because he thought of his family as his own property, while you ran away into a land he could not enter, into the land of art, literature, and of course you have stolen Ottla from him. He will not understand you until death, and after death.

FRANZ. He did not understand me, but he did see through me, and this is a higher form of understanding. I know he never read my books; he would leave them uncut on his night table. Well, instead he read *Ali Baba and the Forty Thieves*. He probably read Dickens, Goethe, and I am sure he read Wilhelm Raabe's *Chronik der Sperlingsgasse* but he never read either you or me. We were not sufficiently mature and I'm sure that if father were to come in here suddenly and shout, "What are you up to boys?" or, "Are you playing naughty games?" I would be petrified and you would faint.

TABLEAU XI

MAX. Nonsense! You're talking rubbish...

FRANZ. But we are playing naughty games! Poets do play naughty games and are ashamed of serious grown-up people because, my dear friend, our writing, when confronted with life, is a shameful, ugly game. Have you had enough or shall we find a vegetarian restaurant? I am now a grass-eating animal except that I drink wine and beer.

MAX. I am not hungry.

FRANZ. Father always sees us as little boys who play at theatre and at writing books but he wasn't fooled, he's seen through us, although you are in a better position, you are almost level with him, you've got married! You don't even realize your great achievement. You're a husband, a male defending the nest, you are baring teeth at each other while I've run away into the corner, my tail between my legs.

MAX. You're pompous and, forgive me, also ridiculous with those remarks about my marriage. Every day, every minute there is a pair coming together, making children. If marriage and copulation were humanity's greatest achievement we would still be waiting for the invention of printing, the steam engine and electricity. It's easier to make a child than to sew a pair of trousers properly and that's why there are now two billion of us, and then there'll be ten and twenty, and then we shall eat each other and there will be peace. You create a mystery out of what is as natural as breathing and defecating. You seduce girls and make women unhappy; you've raised the sexual act to the sphere of the intellect and the mind and that's why you've failed as a lover and a prospective husband. Or maybe you are just being selfish! Let's go to this vegetarian restaurant.

(*FRANZ closes the doors of the stove and switches off the lights. They go out leaving an empty room with a suitcase against the wall*).

TABLEAU XII

At the Barber's

Two mirrors on the wall; washbasins, arm-chairs, cupboards, gleaming scissors, shaving instruments and glass jars. To one side chairs, a coat-hanger and a table. FRANZ covered in a white sheet sits in the armchair, his back to the audience, his face reflected in the mirror. The BARBER has a moustache; he is swarthy, fat and balding. He interrupts the hair-cutting and adjusts FRANZ'S posture with his hands. FRANZ sits with his eyes closed. A young assistant is sweeping the floor, then goes over to a wash-basin, wets his hair, combs it carefully, examines his face, sits down in one of the chairs and starts picking his nose.

BARBER. *(Working up the suds).* Vic! Nose-picking can damage your brain! Run along and get the paper, the world's unhinged and there he sits picking his nose!

VIC. It's my nose...

BARBER. Can you imagine, sir, that this layabout doesn't read newspapers? For us humans it's difficult to understand what's inside those closed minds. Maybe it's not a head, just a cabbage, if you'll excuse a crude expression. Anyway, I read Hlas Naroda, so how can I associate with people without culture or faith? Although I'm totally against class prejudice, nevertheless I can't accept that Vic is equal to me, or, if you allow me, sir, your good self. Stop scratching, you little puppy!

VIC. What else am I to do? I am waiting for the money and you're just carrying on.

BARBER. *(Stops lathering the soap, gives VIC change and sharpens the razor on a belt).* All you can think of is money! Allow me, sir, to congratulate you following the newspaper announcement where I had the pleasure of reading about your engagement to the lady of your heart. As a sincere democrat I am totally opposed to class prejudice, especially in relation to our fair sex. From the bottom of my heart I congratulate you on your choice, sir, as I had the pleasure of combing Miss Slovik's little head. And do believe me, our ladies have no more intimate confessors than in our profession. Indeed a priest or a doctor may hold the secrets of the soul but only the barber is the confessor of, if I may so put it, the whole person, that is, both of the bodily side and of the secrets of the heart, that is of the psyche. Miss Slovik possesses various attributes worthy of your status, and she has that something which only we men value in a woman and without which she may even be an archduchess and possess diadems, fur coats and drawing rooms, and yet remain, as far as we're concerned, a porcelain doll.

(Sounds of a military march. An elegant elderly GENTLEMAN enters; he has a long white beard, wears a black coat, bowler and glasses. He is followed by VIC carrying the newspaper which he places on the table. VIC bows and runs up to the GENTLEMAN who hands him successively the bowler, gloves, walking stick and coat. VIC receives every item with a bow and places them on the hanger. VIC offers the GENTLEMAN an armchair. The GENTLEMAN sits down, moving and adjusting his body for comfort. This whole scene is reflected in the mirror. The BARBER interrupts his work.)

Does your worship desire a hair-wash? If so, this task can be excellently performed by Vic, and when your hair is dry I shall have the pleasure of taking your revered head into my hands... Vic!

(The BARBER resumes shaving. From now on he pays no further attention either to his new client or to VIC's behaviour. FRANZ continues to sit with his eyes shut and the BARBER now covers his face with a wet cloth. FRANZ sits like a manequin. VIC stands behind the GENTLEMAN, awaiting his instructions. The BARBER removes the cloth from FRANZ'S face and begins to lather it.)

Head to the right, please! So, to pick up the thread, a woman who entrusts her little head to us becomes in a certain sense our slave... sweet and compliant... and we become the confessors and trustees before whom a woman opens up the secrets of her little heart. And these women are not just any old *hausfraus*, but ladies with education and frequently from the upper classes. They open up before us like a rose to a butterfly, and often tell us of such matters connected with their material life that even I blush though I am myself a doting husband, and, as they say, a man of the world... to the left now, please... and when the wife tells me openly about her husband's impotence I feel like feigning deafness. I had the honour of learning from our mutual friend that in moments free from more serious engagements you are the author of novels which are approved of even in Vienna. Well sir, I too used to write at school and one of my creations was reprinted in *Kriegs-Echo*.

VIC. *(Presents a choice of coloured towels and cloths to the GENTLEMAN).* Which colour would sir wish, white, red, blue?

GENTLEMAN. The white thank you.

(VIC bends over, the GENTLEMAN whispers something to him, gesticulating. VIC stands over the GENTLEMAN'S chair. Suddenly with a brutal movement he plunges the GENTLEMAN'S head into the wash-basin and holds it there until the GENTLEMAN begins to suffocate. He then pulls the head up by the hair and plunges it into the water once more. The GENTLEMAN is choking.)

TABLEAU XII

What's this, what's this?

(Choking)

I... the police... where's the police?
VIC. *(Pressing him calmly). Mensch... Mensch.*
GENTLEMAN. I...
VIC. *Alte Pipe!*
GENTLEMAN. I...
VIC. *Maul halten!*
GENTLEMAN. I have been decorated with the Iron Cross, second class, and they wrote about me in the *Kriegs-Echo* in August 1915. I have been carrying the cutting here in my wallet against my heart like a relic for the last twenty-five years...

(Impatiently searching his wallet)

Here, read it!

(VIC takes the yellowed cutting)

My name is Friedenthal, Doktor Friedenthal...
VIC. *(Reading with difficulty).* A straw cake... at a teaparty for military doctors in Berlin cakes were served made from flour, derived from straw according to the method of the chemist Professor Doktor Friedenthal. This flour is ground from barley straw. Reporters on Berlin newspapers praised these cakes highly, maintaining that they were tasty, digestible and nourishing. They rest their case on the example of Dr Friedenthal who is of the opinion that for proper digestion the stomach requires some indigestible ballast and that if humans and animals confine themselves wholly to nourishing food they can't maintain their health...

(During the reading the GENTLEMAN looks around proudly, seemingly searching for confirmation of his dignity but the BARBER and FRANZ are motionless, they hear nothing, they see nothing. VIC tears the cutting up into tiny fragments and throws them on the floor)

Scheisse!
GENTLEMAN. *(Jumping from his armchair).* Gentlemen, I protest! Gentlemen, I take you as witnesses!
VIC. *Alte Latrine!* Do you know who is talking to you? The Iron Siegfried is talking to you...
GENTLEMAN. *(Surprised).* The Iron Siegfried?

(Stretches his hand out to VIC. VIC takes the GENTLEMAN'S stick)

VIC. *Alter Hut!*
GENTLEMAN. I...
VIC. *(Pulling the GENTLEMAN's beard). Du alter Pinsel...du...*

(Pointing with the stick)

Get dressed...*los, los,* your bundle!

(Throws down the GENTLEMAN'S coat, bowler, scarf and galoshes)

Pick up your rags! *Los...los!*

(The black wall parts revealing a twilight area illuminated by one bulb over a chair. VIC pushes the GENTLEMAN towards the darkness with his stick. At this moment the barber resumes his energetic activities continuing to shave FRANZ.)

BARBER. I venture to assert that we barbers, and also tailors and shoemakers, understand the souls of our female clients better than the renowned poets, for what can a poet grasp of female mystery? Only the soul or the intelligence, but a woman knows that her hairstyle, her dress, her perfume, her shoes, her stockings, and not her soul, tempt the butterfly or in this case the man. Like the corolla of a flower which opens out its bud in order to attract an insect to its honey; well, that's how the world is organised and a poet or a writer like any other man gets caught by these colours and scents, these fripperies and baubles, and moves blindly to the cup of nectar...Vic, where is the cologne bottle?

(He interrupts the shaving in order to sharpen his razor on the belt)

Vic, you wretch! Do forgive me, sir, but one can never find that wretch when he is needed...

(At the same time, while the barber is talking to FRANZ, in the darkness behind the black wall, which is still split open, the scene continues between VIC and the GENTLEMAN—the two scenes are parallel. The light behind the black wall grows, the light in the BARBER'S shop fades.

VIC. *(Pushing the GENTLEMAN with his stick).* And now get undressed! This is a body search. Stack your things on the left. Take everything off and pile it up.

(The GENTLEMAN takes off his clothes, shoes, stockings and underclothes and stacks everything by the chair)

Open your trap!

TABLEAU XII

(VIC pokes his fingers in the GENTLEMAN'S mouth, pushes him onto the chair, searches between his fingers and toes, behind his ears and under his tongue. He is now holding a shiny nickel-plated hair-cutter.)

Now through the middle of your head we'll create a beautiful *Lauspromenade*... three fingers wide. There, you look beautiful with that parting, the lice will have somewhere to walk. And now, get dressed! These are your things... Los! Los!

(With the stick he pokes through a pile of rags and shoes and throws a selection towards the GENTLEMAN. The GENTLEMAN puts on a nightshirt, a lady's torn green sweater, old ragged trousers and shoes; one is a big boot with long laces and other a small lady's shoe; he also puts on a white armband with the Star of David.)

VIC. *(standing aside)*. Raus! Raus!

(With his stick he pushes the GENTLEMAN who quickly passes through the BARBER'S shop, stumbling, and leaves through the door. VIC goes over to the mirror, inspects his face and combs his hair. The black wall closes.)

BARBER. Vic, stop picking your nose, you'll damage your brain! There you are, you drone, you haven't even glanced at the paper... allow me, sir.

(Gently places two fingers around FRANZ's nose and raises it slightly)

Well sir, if you can imagine this drone...
VIC. I am not curious about papers.
BARBER. Just imagine it, sir, this lout doesn't read papers... but we well-read people find it hard to understand what's inside those blocks.
VIC. *(Picks up the paper and mumbles to himself)*. Dum... dum... ultimutum.
BARBER. See how he stutters. Well, what have you read there, you mad buffoon?
VIC. We have declared war on Serbia.
BARBER. *(Shudders and scratches FRANZ'S cheek)*. My heartiest apologies. Well, really! My hand shook... we'll stop the bleeding at once... at once... Vic, where is that jar of alum... next time give us a bit of warning... I am shaving a gentleman and he says "War's broken out"... we'll have it disinfected immediately... the wound is quite superficial... and all because of that idiot! Literally only a drop of blood, a million apologies.

(Bathes the wound in alum and then with eau de cologne, blows dry and sticks on a plaster)

My heartfelt apologies but this news came so suddenly...

THE TRAP

(The BARBER hands FRANZ the newspaper and FRANZ reads it)

We are finishing this instant. I do hope the gentleman doesn't find the wound troublesome.

(Showers FRANZ'S face with an atomiser and dries it with a towel. Sounds of a military march. The music dies away and as the lights fade the EXECUTIONERS remove all stage props. VIC sweeps away the hair.)

TABLEAU XIII

Go and see her

A room with an alcove and a screen with Chinese decorations. The room is simply furnished. A picture on the wall. A boy of about 10 or 12 is sitting at table, he is big and fat with a huge overblown and deformed head. His face is covered with thick black down. He emits grunts and squeals; he is deaf and dumb. Beside him a young fair-haired woman holds a coloured brick in her hand. There is a pyramid of these bricks on the table. A fruit bowl stands between the boy and the young woman; it's filled with noodles or porridge. The woman places the brick on top of the pyramid, takes a spoon, dips it in the bowl, tastes it, smacks her lips, signifying the food is good and moves the spoon to the boy's lips. The boy sits motionless without opening his mouth. The food dribbles down his chin which the woman wipes with a napkin: she picks up another spoonful, the boy turns his head showing his gritted teeth, the woman attempts various other forms of feeding, at last she puts the spoon away and sits in silence, supporting her head with her hands and then pulls the bowl towards her.

GRETE. My little boy doesn't want to eat... my little boy is naughty... doggie will eat everything, won't he?

(She puts the bowl under the table. The boy grabs the bricks and throws them on the floor, one of them falling into the bowl. He squats by the bowl, eats noisily from it, lifts the bowl, licks it and throws it away. Sitting under the table and taking no notice of his mother, he takes off his shoe and examines it carefully. GRETE pulls away the screen, revealing a bed, a chest and some toys under the bed, a bowl on a stool, a towel and a jug of water. She pulls the boy from under the table, undresses him, washes his face and hands, tucks him up in bed under an eiderdown and pulls the screen across. She sings a lullaby in a beautiful clear voice.)

Schlaf, Püppchen, schlaf!
Da draussen gehen die Schaf,
die schwarzen und nie weissen,
die wolln mein Püppchen beissen...

(Suddenly strange noises, mumblings and squeals begin to mingle with the song... animal snorts... silence... then sounds of a tussle, the sound of a falling body, cries of pain, then silence... heavy breathing, then silence which lasts for a

whole minute, then again spasmodic quickened breathing. GRETE enters the room, her blouse is torn, her hair dishevelled, her face scratched, she licks her lips as though licking off blood. She stands in the middle of the room, walks up to the mirror, combs her hair, listens but there is silence behind the screen. She dabs her face with eau de cologne, opens a wardrobe, puts on a dark dress, examines herself in the mirror. Clears the table. There is a ring at the door and MAX enters wearing a light raincoat and carrying a heavy black suitcase. He stands at the door clutching the suitcase.)

MAX. I am sorry I'm late.
GRETE. Oh, it's you...please don't apologise; just as well you are late... please put the suitcase down.
MAX. I saw him...
GRETE. I'm listening.
MAX. He is dying.
GRETE. Dying he travels, he writes, he even gets engaged! For someone on his deathbed he leads quite a varied life while we who are healthy, we healthy women lead a much less attractive life...please go on...
MAX. He gave me no message, no letter...he said go and see her...he was feverish and had a small haemorrhage...these words flowed out of his lips together with the blood...I asked what I was to tell you...he looked long into my eyes, then turned to the wall and said once more, "Go and see her"...and didn't speak again.

(MAX compulsively fidgets with his glasses and wipes them, smiles at GRETE and makes a resigned gesture with his hands)

GRETE. And what did you see?!
MAX. The doctors give him two or three months...but he may die sooner.. I bade him farewell...but he has now regained hope and is making plans...says he likes his beer...I was in Berlin several days, there was some improvement, he started going out for walks...his book has appeared there. I have a few copies with me...despite his weakness and the haemorrhage he was pleased at the sight of this little book...if you are interested...

(GRETE is silent)

Do you ever see Felice?
GRETE. We write occasionally.
MAX. Once more, apologies for imposing on you...I myself don't see the point...sometimes a soldier doesn't understand the command and yet must obey.

(Behind the screen sounds of stirring and heavy breathing)

GRETE. Would you like some tea?

TABLEAU XIII

MAX. *(Listening to the whimpering and breathing behind the screen).* Yes please, that would be very nice.

(MAX gives the screen a worried look and then watches GRETE. GRETE leaves the room. MAX takes off his coat, places it on top of the suitcase, and walks about the room, moves over to the screen, listens, there is silence. GRETE brings in a tea-set which she arranges on the table.)

GRETE. Have some tea.
MAX. Could I be of help in any way?
GRETE. Thank you.
MAX. I am his friend...maybe he thought you were short of money... please be absolutely honest with me.
GRETE. *(Smiles).* Absolutely? Well...I have a job, I have enough to eat as you can see, I have a flat...please write to him...that I think warmly of him and wish him a speedy recovery.
MAX. Naturally, I'll send off a telegram immediately saying that I have seen you and that you are sending him your heartfelt greetings.

(Takes off his glasses and polishes them)

GRETE. As you wish.
MAX. I have complied with the patient's request...I am his closest friend.
GRETE. You think so?

(MAX looks surprised)

He is your best friend? Can he be a friend?
MAX. Yes.
GRETE. Has he ever told you that he is your friend...he always said that you are his friend...but did he say that he is your friend?!
MAX. One doesn't say such things.
GRETE. Doesn't one? You're saying it.

(Smiles at MAX)

MAX. You know...it's only women who declare friendship and love to each other. From morning till night they assure each other of love and friendship..., they do it several times a day...men never talk of friendship or love...or perhaps only once...when they part forever or in the face of death...
GRETE. *(Smiling).* Or when one of the friends gets married.

(There is a stirring behind the screen. MAX gives GRETE a worried look.)

Ah, please take no notice. It's only a little dog, it's got pneumonia, the poor beast, it's asleep and it's having bad dreams. You are married, I can tell by the ring, but did you ask your best friend for permission to get married?

MAX. I don't understand.

GRETE. Hadn't you discussed with him your plans, you intentions, your fiancée?

MAX. He had no objections... I had the impression that he was pleased.

GRETE. You had "an impression", and hadn't you by any chance noticed your best friend's expression when you told him that you were getting married?

MAX. I can't remember... I think he was somewhat amused... I don't recollect his expression.

GRETE. It's a pity you don't remember. I confess, I too hadn't seen our friend's face at that moment either, but I can imagine what he looked like when happy and excited you were telling him about your fiancée, the wedding, the presents and your honeymoon. You've had your honeymoon, and I too once dreamed of it, what a beautiful word it is—honey-moon, honey... this word is so warm, sweet, gooey, golden, aromatic.

MAX. *(Smiling).* I don't understand what my honeymoon has to do with our friend. You're pulling my leg.

GRETE. God forbid! I'm convinced you are a gourmet... watching your lips... women can instinctively tell a gourmet... and looking at you I know that you've not only had the honey but also licked the vessel to the very bottom. How pleasant it is when the bride takes over from overworked hands.

(GRETE smiles)

Please don't be angry, you are nice... I am not a good hostess; have some jam, it's home-made. A wasted talent, I was an excellent cook and wife, but your best friend bolted, that is, ran away. First he ran away from Felice, then he ran away from a few others. Poor Felice, she held him twice but the bird flew away. Herr Doktor got frightened by the wardrobe and the bed. Felice told me about it but I had forgotten. Furniture, wardrobes, terrify him. Felice tried to understand that, she cried, she tried to explain; I also cried! Do you like this jam? I laughed and cried!

(MAX watches GRETE)

My friend... quite so! Observing you I see a good husband who doesn't run away but who weaves a nest for the young with his chosen female. You are a flirtatious darting little sparrow. As for him, he must be a black crow, a silent crow. Are you still listening to me? Thank you. Nowadays nobody listens to anyone else. That's not your fault... what can one nothing tell another nothing... I suppose people don't listen much in the theatre either, even when it's Shakespeare or Schiller. People listen for only a moment and then they just stare, waiting for something to happen. You are a funny bird! All this time I have the feeling you are eavesdropping and not listening. You think I am a stupid gasbag, but I have suffered, so I'll tell you little stories about birds. You bring feathers, straws and coins into the nest. First she brings a straw, then he brings a feather, she brings a wardrobe, you bring a bed, she brings a table, you an article, she a sofa, you a short story, she an eiderdown, you a picture, she a vase, you flowers...

(Grasps MAX by the hand)

...while our crow preferred death to Felice and not only that...he preferred illness to family life...he was drawn to the female, seeking shelter in the cosy armpit but he was scared of wardrobes and he was also scared of me! So instead of a nest I have nothing; he wanted warmth and left me cold.

(GRETE laughs)

MAX. You'll wake...

(Looks towards the screen)

GRETE. It won't be waking up anyone, I told you, it's a sick little dog, and I sometimes wonder whether to put him to sleep. Don't get up! If you've been sent on a mission don't run away. "Go and see her;" you haven't seen anything yet and already your legs are trembling with fear and you want to run away to your wifie and tell her everything in bed, in the downy marital nest. You'll tell her about that mad Grete who's been left holding the baby, because now the other one is dying, your wife will become your best friend. It will be more convenient like this because even in bed you will be able to tell your new friend who is so sweet, so soft, and compliant, about a friend who is departing to the next world. In a word, do you understand me?

MAX. I'll go now...

GRETE. But what if I won't let you go? You're easily scared but I have a way of keeping you here. As you can see, I live here like a nun but I'm quite all right, aren't I? I've noticed the greedy look with which you've fondled my breasts, my thighs and my bottom...

(GRETE listens to the heavy breathing, disappears behind the screen for a moment)

Quiet doggie, quiet little doggie.

(Comes out again. At this moment MAX is helping himself to more jam and is startled, as though caught red-handed. GRETE looks at him, smiling. She sits down and they stay silent. The silence is prolonged. GRETE covers her face with her hands.)

So you can't recall your friend's look... you can't remember the expression on your best friend's face when you said you were getting married. And, without being asked, you started telling him what your fiancée looked like and then when you returned from your honeymoon you told him about the Italian lakes and he listened and was a little amused, but unfortunately you were deaf and blind. All covered with honey you went to him happy, sweet and sticky with your happiness, so you didn't notice the expression of disgust on his face. You noticed nothing? But I can see, even though I wasn't there, how he surreptitiously wiped his palms when you kept grabbing his hands, talking ecstatically about the journey. And don't feel guilty about liking jam; grown-ups too can have a sweet tooth, my dear Alphonse!

MAX. I have always been called Max, and I am at your service...

GRETE. As far as I am concerned you are Alphonse. Please don't be angry... this soft name is more suitable to your role and even your figure...

MAX. As you wish, madam...

GRETE. Well Alphonse, you're an envoy, a messsenger, a go-between, a deputy, and everything else but not a friend. He used you like an artificial limb to touch certain problems in life which caused him disgust and fear. Don't you remember, you were the messenger of love to that Swiss girl? Then there was the daughter of that cobbler, I can't remember her name. The last one probably was the fiancée, that most serious candidate for a wife, and the last. I'll give you another portion of the jam, I'll give you the lot if you tell me about the courtship between the poet and the cobbler's daughter who is a dishwasher.

MAX. *(Gets up, buttons up his jacket, gets the buttons wrong so that the jacket stands up crookedly, unbuttons the coat and buttons it up again correctly).* No. I won't tell you, he is dying and there is nothing here to laugh about.

GRETE. But I am crying, can't you see that. Well, go... you're blind... please go.

TABLEAU XIV

He will never grow up

Years later. The dining room in the parents' apartment. The same furnishings with the same table and chairs. A weak light. FRANZ and MOTHER are sitting at the table. There is a bowl of soup on the table and two places set. FRANZ lifts his spoon regularly in silence. On the wall opposite FRANZ there is a huge portrait of the FATHER. It's a poorly painted picture of a man in middle age wearing his Sunday best; he has a moustache, large eyes and closely cropped hair. FRANZ glances at MOTHER, lifts his eyes to the portrait and stops eating. He smiles and points to the painting with his finger.

FRANZ. "Vereidigter Sachverständiger bei Gerichte."
MOTHER. It was me... it was my birthday present for him. I commissioned a painting based on an old photograph. To tell you the truth that painter skinned me, but you must agree, it's a good portrait. Several times I caught father looking at himself with pleasure... don't you like the soup, Franz?
FRANZ. It's very tasty, I love celery soup, it's absolutely wonderful. But mother, you're staring at me and not eating anything yourself.

(MOTHER watches her son in silence and with the same old shy, tender movement she strokes his hand)

After dinner I'd like to talk to father... I'd like to communicate to you and him... that is... I'd like to have your consent to my marriage with Miss Jana Slovik... to whom I got engaged a week ago... I had not informed both of you earlier as I wasn't certain of the consent of the young lady and her parents.

(MOTHER wants to say something but stops herself)

I am sure of your consent because I am certain of your love... but I don't know how father will react.
MOTHER. I don't know, I am scared... he thinks you are making a fool of him with all these engagements and announcements you concoct to make him a laughing stock and to compromise him in the eyes of acquaintances, friends and enemies. He wept once.
FRANZ. I... mother...

THE TRAP

MOTHER. *(Puts her finger to her lips).* Don't speak so loudly. He is sleeping, he is ill and he musn't be upset.

FRANZ. *(Terrified).* Ill...?

MOTHER. Yesterday when he got back from work he said nothing, he didn't eat. He sat there and didn't reply to my questions. In the night he spoke in his sleep a bit, he was feverish and this morning he didn't have his breakfast and he wouldn't eat lunch. You know what that means, when father refuses to eat. Even when war was declared he ate a hearty breakfast, so by then I was really scared. When I asked whether he was going to the works he just said abruptly, "No," and when I said, "Is there anything the matter?" he just didn't reply at all, then he shut himself in his room and I stood outside listening, but there was no sound. And then I heard him cry in a terrible voice, "I'll tear him apart like a frog," so I asked him whether he was calling me, whether he needed anything and asked him to open, but he was quiet then so I went in and there he was sitting up fully dressed and staring at me as if I were a stranger. So again I asked him to eat something but he said he had to go out immediately, but he just sat there motionless, so I put him in bed and he is asleep now.

FRANZ. I suspect that illness has something to so with my engagement. It's a form of protest, it's to do with my fiancée. I should have been torn apart like a frog immediately after my birth or when I was six! Now I am a high official, a doctor of laws, and a respected writer. I now have a large furnished apartment...why hadn't he torn me apart earlier...?

(FRANZ talks loudly, MOTHER looks at him terrified and covers her mouth with her hand)

I must see him, I suspect he is simulating illness to avoid talking to me. I'd better go to him.

(FRANZ gets up)

MOTHER. *(Grasps his arm).* Wait, let me go first, I'll prepare him...I'll see, perhaps he's awake now...I'll tell him you have important business with him...or won't it be better if I prepare him today and you go in tomorrow? Then the news won't be so sudden...father is no longer strong.

FRANZ. No, mother, I must talk to him now alone. He isn't ill...he is playing a comedy...he tortures you because you are the only one left...I suspect he's eavesdropping.

MOTHER. You musn't talk like that about father. He always loved you all...and really this is all he ever had apart from work. Maybe this wasn't a subtle, bookish love. Just simply he loved, and so he worked to maintain us and looked after us. And so what if he couldn't talk elegantly like your friends, the actors and writers? You are unjust; he too needs affection and warmth. He also suffers, even though he doesn't write endlessly about it...oh, I am sorry...

(MOTHER covers her face with her hands)

I won't judge either of you because I love you both, but I am now very tired...of everything...even my love.
FRANZ. This time, I'll do it myself...this time you will not be a go-between or a patron of matrimonial plans. Father is putting up this show because he knows something. I won't whisper; I'll shout!

(FRANZ says this almost in a whisper)

All these years you've stood between us with your love torn in two, and now your "Child of sorrow" is grown up. This will be a conversation between two grown men. All I ask you to do is to wake father up and warn him I am about to see him. You could tell him that my book has appeared, that you wish to give him a copy, though he once made it clear to me he has no time for reading.

(Suddenly a door opens in the black wall. FATHER appears in a glaring light. He has changed a lot; he is wearing the old suit in the portrait which is now too large for him, he looks like a boy who has put on his elder brother's clothes. He has shrunk and dried up and even his head looks smaller, so that the bowler rests on his big ears. Only the moustache has remained bushy and black, turned up provocatively. FATHER walks up to MOTHER and kisses her forehead.)

FATHER. I am off, I need some air!
FRANZ. Father...

(FATHER pretends not to notice FRANZ...looks around puzzled...wants to go but FRANZ steps in front of him)

Father!
FATHER. Ah, it's you!
FRANZ. I've brought you a little book, it's just appeared.
FATHER. Hear that?! He's brought me his little book.
FRANZ. Father, please sit down and have dinner with us.

(Puts the book on the table)

FATHER. But make it snappy, I am in a hurry, I also have my business.
MOTHER. Please Hermann...please sit down...have something to eat...I'm sorry.

(FATHER sits down beneath his portrait)

THE TRAP

FRANZ. I'd like to ask you... I'd like to let you know.
FATHER. *(Waves his hand).* I know everything.

(Turns to MOTHER)

He must be inviting us to his latest engagement and to meet the family of the "fiancée!"

(MOTHER places a plate in front of FATHER, ladles soup from the bowl. She appears nervous, smiling faintly at FRANZ and at FATHER. FATHER sits at table with his bowler still on.)

Are the announcements and invitations printed? Have you settled the wedding reception menu? Do you know your fiancée's name? So there he is, come to make an "announcement." Well, my dear sir, you ought to know that yesterday evening the father of your dishwashing maid announced your sweet secret to all the guests gathered at *The Duck's Arse*. He kept communicating this throughout the evening to all the guests both drunk and sober, to his friends and casual listeners. He spent the whole evening entertaining them all about an engagement "per procura" of his daughter to a procurer and, as cobblers have a better sense of humour than clerks and writers, he embellished his tale with various funny and juicy expressions. He had an appreciative audience of his theatrical performance. You know the theatre better than I do, so you would really have had a laugh watching your father-in-law. The show lasted till midnight.

(FATHER takes off his bowler and wipes his brow with an handkerchief)

I left the hostelry during a break, just as the cobbler was re-enacting the scene when your fully authorized messenger was praising your virtues to your fiancée's parents. I must admit he portrayed your friend Max splendidly. When he started fidgetting, rubbing his little glasses, lisping, straining his eyes, unbuttoning and buttoning his flies, when he started spitting and neighing and salivating and squeaking with his unbroken voice, people were rolling in the aisles. I too couldn't help smiling even though I had my back turned to the whole show because it looked as though our brave little cobbler might stand me a beer and start being familiar. A cabbie there had a high opinion of the show and yelled at me: "You could piss yourself laughing."

(FRANZ gets up, sits; for a moment FRANZ and FATHER watch each other in silence)

And now he wants to "communicate"... you could piss yourself laughing.
FRANZ. Father...I...

TABLEAU XIV

FATHER. Do what you like, you're grown up...
FRANZ. Father...

(MOTHER leaves, covering her face)

FATHER. And I? And I, sonny?
FRANZ. Father...I...
FATHER. He starts everything with "I"...I, I, I...can't you ever cough up "we"?

(FRANZ picks up the book which he had brought for his father, leafs through it and reads. Behind the wall there are sounds of heavy footsteps, cries and curses. The wall opens and two men with a huge wardrobe squeeze themselves in. It's the same wardrobe that the engaged couple, FRANZ and FELICE, were inspecting years ago in the furniture store. FATHER runs around the men, mounts a chair and takes down his portrait, his likeness being larger than in real life. He walks around the stage holding the portrait.)

Put this wardrobe against the wall...or perhaps in the corner...yes, it will be better in the corner...

(The men set down the wardrobe and FATHER hands them small coins. FATHER looks inside the wardrobe while the men look around the room.)

Thank you, gentlemen, and goodbye! You know the way out.

(The men don't listen to FATHER. One has opened his huge palm and is examining the tiny coin, while the other is walking around the room, looks at the china in the sideboard, feels the carpet and stops in front of FATHER's portrait, then walks up to his colleague, whispers into his ear, while the other shakes his head and shrugs his shoulders. Then they both leave the room, laughing. The black wall closes and the sound of laughter fading in the distance can still be heard. FRANZ, absorbed in his book, has not noticed the men. He closes the book and weighs it in his hand.)

FRANZ. This is *A Letter to his Father*.
FATHER. What letter...whose father?
FRANZ. This is my letter to you.
FATHER. Your letter? Letter? What have you thought of this time? Don't bother about books and letters to me. I have no time for your inventions and laments. I have the whole family on my head...where to hide them all...

(Opens the wardrobe)

how many people can get in...

(Enters the wardrobe)

standing? Or sitting...after all I can't keep standing all the time! And we need some grub and water, blankets and coats. How many of us could get in here? Mother? Me? Valli with her husband and the brats; that makes five, no, that's already seven, and what about grandpa and grandma? Grandpa has to sit down so we need a chair...any minute now they'll be here!

FRANZ. Dad.

FATHER. *(Speaks from inside the wardrobe).* Dad...dad...mum...you are a doctor of law but you can't figure things out. You don't see anything, you hear nothing: it's intelligence that makes people stupid. Uncle Alfred has sent a telegram from Madrid that he is coming to our silver wedding, presumably with all his medals and his automobile. He too is a clever fool; will your excellency step into the wardrobe? And no doubt your beloved Uncle Siegfried will arrive on horseback so I'll ask the horse in as well.

(FATHER steps out of the wardrobe)

I am a simple man, a simple merchant, my father was a butcher, he couldn't read or write but he knew how to live and die. And what do you know? You with your titles, you and your literary gents, the philosophers and the doctors...you don't even know whether you are alive or dead. You remember that friend of yours, what was his name? Lissauer...the things he used to write during the First World War, how stupid he was! And the other one, a doctor like you, Herr Doktor Hugo Zuckermann...and do you remember what he used to write? He published a poem, I remember it well, this poem by Zuckermann, it was called *Oesterreichisches Reiterlied*, that's what is was called, and now I will recite it to you and you'll listen.

(FATHER stands to attention by his portrait and recites)

Drüber am Wiesenrand
Hocken zwei Dohlen
Fall ich am Donaustrand?
Fall ich in Polen?
Was liegt daran?
Ehe, sie meine Seele holen
Kämpf ich als Reitersman.
Drüber am Ackerrein
Schreien zwei Raben
Werd ich der erste sein,
Den sie begraben?
Was ist dabei?
Viel Hunderttausend traben

TABLEAU XIV

In Oesterreichs Reiterei.
Drüber im Abendrot
Fliegen zwei Krähen
Wann kommt der Schnitter Tod,
Um uns zu mähen?
Es ist nicht schad!
Seh ich nur unsere Fahnen wehen
Auf Belgrad!

"I see our flags flying over Belgrade!" But tell me Amschel, what has Zuckermann to do with Belgrade? You are poets and scholars and we are nothing. Why must Doktor Zuckermann have his flag waving over Belgrade? Because he is an Austrian cavalryman?! And that other chap, Lissauer... what has he got against England? And I am just that stupid shopkeeper Dohle Zuckermann writes about. But I must hide in the wardrobe.

(FATHER pulls out the lower drawer and attempts to stretch himself inside it)

FRANZ. Dad.

(Kneels by the drawer)

What are you doing in that drawer? You are delirious... you're ill!

(Touches his brow with his hand)

FATHER. You ask about me and the wardrobe? Fool! Is that wardrobe in your way? Everything was always in your way. I know your letters to Felice... she read them all to me...

(FATHER imitates FRANZ's voice)

"Ah Felice, ah Felice, oh Felice, so we are setting up house! You're right Felice, our furniture ought to be solid, so heavy that no one can shift it..."

(FATHER gets up)

"You wish to see me snug and cosy! You want solid furniture, massive wardrobes, heavy sideboards and a marital bed! Solidity is what you value most... solidity of people and furniture."

(FATHER runs around the wardrobe, touching it with his hand)

"But do you know, Felice, this sideboard presses on my chest, this wardrobe is like a colossal stone on my grave, it is the grave and gravestone of my clerking life? You are inspecting furniture while I hear funeral bells...."

THE TRAP

(FATHER stops before FRANZ, touching FRANZ's chest with his index finger)

Tfu! *Myschygene!* The tears that girl wept because you've made so much fun of the furniture, that poor child cried because you fancied that a bed is not necessary, that a sideboard is a gravestone pressing on your chest! And that from a grown up, educated man... shame on you! Don't you know that a wardrobe like this can save the life of your mother and your grandmother, and your grandfather and your sisters with their husbands and brats, your Uncle Siegfried with his horse and your father? But what do you care about your family? What do you know about life? You are no better as prophet than Zuckermann was as a cavalry man! Your sister Ottla and the woman Milena... they will have to go through it... go and ask them. They will die in that hell. You don't need the wardrobe, you don't need the bed, you can live in a lair, in a shelter, because you are a badger, a rat. Don't you enter our wardrobe—because you hate human and family warmth! Build yourself a shelter in the earth in a field somewhere or in a forest... Quiet!

(FATHER presses a finger to his lips and then tries to burrow under the carpet. One can see his thin legs protruding under his trousers. FRANZ tries to pull him out but he hisses and squeals like an animal. Then FRANZ pulls back the carpet and FATHER rolls on his back, lying defenceless, his arms and legs stretched upwards. FRANZ bends over and picks FATHER up in his arms. FATHER's face twists in a grimace or smile, he is counting the buttons on his jacket. He pulls out a watch on a chain and listens to it... He is behaving like a little child. The black wall parts and a sharp light falls on a bed piled high with cushions and an eiderdown. This is the room of JOSIE, the maidservant. FRANZ tucks FATHER under the eiderdown and sits on the edge of the bed.)

FRANZ. Lie quietly, I'll go and fetch the doctor. Have a nap and don't worry, dad. You'll enjoy a long life; you'll bury me and the stone you'll place over my grave will be so massive I won't be able to lift it.

FATHER. *(Sits up)*. Amschel... why don't you listen to your father for once? You are a blind rat and deaf as a doorknob. You can't see that pack of hounds running all over, through villages and towns, through forests and streets, you don't hear their yapping, but I with my wretched peasant's nose which sniffs the ground and the trees and bread and meat, can smell them on our tracks. They will find us above the earth and under the earth, and they will find you in your shelter. They'll strangle and burn us all. They'll find you in the cellar and under the bed, in the wardrobe and in the wall. The best thing you can do, Amschel, is to go into the country, to Uncle Siegfried: on horseback he looks like a baron. Or go to Ottla and dig yourself a lair under that old tree but make sure you have two or three exits away from the lair because the dogs will be searching, they have good scent.

TABLEAU XIV

(FATHER listens attentively)

They are coming already ... they are coming for us ...

(The black wall closes slowly)

TABLEAU XV

Under the wall

The stage is empty, the black wall at the back. Spotlights criss-cross the stage and people begin to emerge singly from the darkness. They are all the characters who took part in the story. Actors are holding hands, approach the footlights, retire, actors bowing to the public while someone presents them with a basket of flowers—a white card is attached to it. Very slowly the black wall begins to part and the EXECUTIONERS enter the stage. They mingle with the actors, calling to each other, and eventually begin to push the people in the direction of the black wall. They push them like cattle into a goods wagon. They press and squeeze them hard into the space. One can see faces and hands... an EXECUTIONER throws in the basket of flowers... the black wall closes slowly, one can still see hands and fingers. The EXECUTIONERS go away. The wall is closed. The wall of death.

ANIMULA stands against the wall. It's an emaciated little boy in a pair of old-fashioned swimming shorts down to its knees. It stands and stares dumbly at the audience. It leaves with the last member of the audience.

Wrocław, 1979–1982

2. *The Trap*, world première at Den Nationale Scene, Bergen, Norway, 15 October 1983, directed by Krystyna Skuszanka, sets and costumes by Krzysztof Pankiewicz, translated by Ole Michael Selberg. Thor Hjorth-Jenssen: Father, Bentein Baardson: Franz. Photo: Trygve Schønfelder

3. *The Trap*, Theatre Studio, Warsaw, director and designer: Jerzy Grzegorzewski, costumes: Barbara Hanicka, première 15 January 1984. Olgierd Łukaszewicz (right). Photo: Wojciech Plewiński.

4. *The Trap*, Theatre Studio, Warsaw, director and designer: Jerzy Grzegorzewski, costumes: Barbara Hanicka, première 15 January 1984. Photo: Wojciech Plewiński.

5. *The Trap*, Theatre Studio, Warsaw, director and designer: Jerzy Grzegorzewski, costumes: Barbara Hanicka, première 15 January 1984. From left to right: Weronika Pawłowska, Olgierd Łukaszewicz, Elżbieta Kijowska. Photo: Wojciech Plewiński.

6. *The Trap*, Teatr Wybrzeże, Gdańsk, directed by Krzysztof Babicki, design by Marian Kołodziej, première 20 May 1984. Krzysztof Gordon: Franz, Sławomira Kozieniec: Animula. Photo: Tadeusz Link.

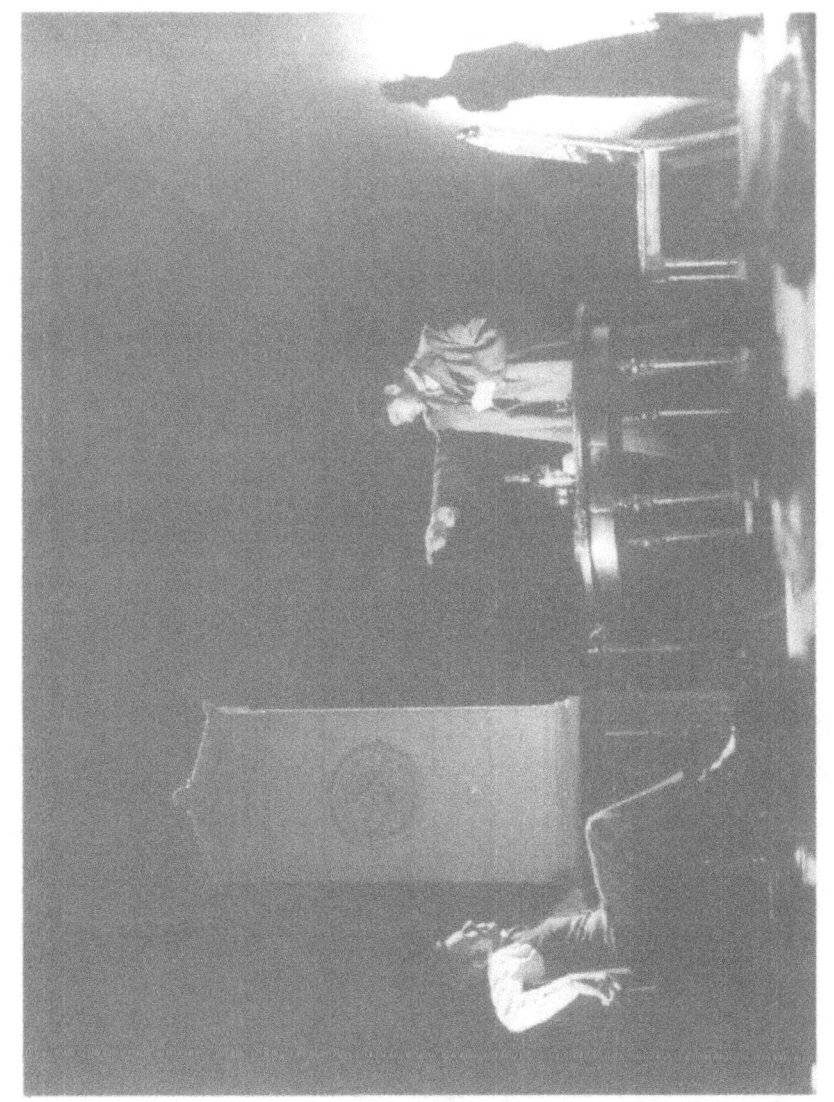

7. *The Trap*, Maxim Gorki Theater, East Berlin, directed by Rolf Winkelgrund, design: Henning Schaller, translated by Henryk Bereska, première 26 September 1985. Jörg Gudzuhn: Franz (left), Uwe Kockisch: Max (right). Photo courtesy of the theatre.

8. *The Trap*, Serbian National Theatre, Novi Sad, Yugoslavia, directed by Nevena Janać, designed by Zofia de Ines-Lewczuk, translated by Petar Vujčić, première 11 February 1988. Stevan Gardinovacki: Father, Ksenija Martinov Pavlovic: Mother, Predrag Ejdus: Franz. Photo: Branislav Lučić.

9. *The Trap*, Wiener Festwochen. Co-production of Wiener Festwochen and Teatr Studio, directed and designed by Jerzy Grzegorzewski, première 5 June 1991. Krystyna Kozanecka: Valli, Tadeusz Łomnicki: Father. Photo: Sergiusz Sachno.

10. *The Trap*, Teatr Polski, Wrocław, director Jerzy Jarocki, designer Jerzy Juk-Kowarski, première 30 May 1992. Edwin Petrykat: Father, Olgierd Łukaszewicz: Franz. Photo: Stefan Okołowicz.

SELECTIVE BIBLIOGRAPHY

(i) Różewicz's Plays, Poetry and Prose in English Translation

The Card Index and Other Plays [*Gone out* and *The Interrupted Act*], tr. Adam Czerniawski. London: Calder and Boyars, 1969.
Faces of Anxiety, tr. Adam Czerniawski. London: Rapp and Whiting, 1969.
The Witnesses and Other Plays [*The Funny Old Man* and *The Old Woman Broods*], tr. Adam Czerniawski. London: Calder and Boyars, 1970.
Selected Poems, tr. Adam Czerniawski. Harmondsworth: Penguin, 1976.
"The Survivor" *and Other Poems*, tr. Magnus J. Krynski and Robert A. Maguire. Princeton, N.J.: Princeton University Press, 1976.
Birth Rate, tr. Daniel Gerould, in *Twentieth-Century Polish Avant-Garde Drama*. Ithaca, N.Y.: Cornell University Press, 1977.
Unease, tr. Victor Contoski. St, Paul; Minnesota: New Rivers Press, 1980.
"In the Most Beautiful City in the World", tr. Adam Czerniawski, *Introduction to Modern Polish Literature*, eds. Adam Gillon and Krystyna Olszer, Hippocrene Books, New York 1982.
Conversations with the Prince and Other Poems, tr. Adam Czerniawski. London: Anvil Press, 1982; revised edition, as *They Came to See a Poet*, 1991.
"Boobsie Tootsie, or Romantic Love is Already Waiting at the Door", "The Double", "A Discordant Drama", and "What Comes What Goes", tr. E. J. Czerwinski, *Slavic and East European Arts*, I, 2 (Spring 1983), 134–49.
Mariage Blanc and The Hunger Artist Departs, tr. Adam Czerniawski. London: Marion Boyars, 1983.
"An Excursion to the Museum", tr. Jadwiga Kosicka, *Formations*, III, 2 (Fall 1936), 85–91.
Tadeusz Różewicz's Bas Relief and Other Poems, tr. Edward Czerwinski. Stony Brook, N.Y.: Slavic Cultural Center Press, 1991.
Forms in relief and other works, tr. Richard Sokoloski. N.Y.: Legas, 1994.
Selected Poems, tr. Adam Czerniawski. Kraków: Wydawnictwo Literackie, 1994.
"The Tip", tr. George Hyde, *The Eagle and the Crow*, eds. George Hyde and Teresa Halikowska, Serpent's Tail, London 1995.

(ii) Critical Studies of Różewicz as a Playwright

Kazimierz Braun and Tadeusz Różewicz *Języki teatru*, Wrocław, 1989.
Stanisław Burkot, *Tadeusz Różewicz*, Warsaw, 1991.

SELECTIVE BIBLIOGRAPHY

Halina Filipowicz, *The Theatre of Subversion, Tadeusz Różewicz as a Playwright*, Columbus, Ohio, 1991.

——, "Theatrical Reality in the Plays of Tadeusz Różewicz", *Slavic and East European Journal*, Vol. 26, No. 4 (1982), 447–59.

——, *A Laboratory of Impure Forms*, Greenwood Press, New York 1991.

Stanisław Gębala, *Teatr Różewicza*, Wrocław, 1977.

Daniel Gerould, "Laocoon at the Frontier, or the Limit of Limits", *Modern Drama*, XXIX: 1 (March 1986): 23–40.

Jóref Kelera, "Leżący pod ścianą", in *Kpiarze i moraliści*, Kraków, 1966.

——, "Od *Kartoteki* do *Pułapki*", in Tadeusz Różewicz, *Teatr*, Vol. 1, Kraków, 1988.

——, "The Różewicz Theatre", *Theatre in Poland*, 10 (October 1975), pp. 7–16.

Jan Kott, "A Very Polish *Card Index*", in *Theatre Notebook 1947–1967* Garden City, New Jersey, 1968.

Notatnik Teatralny (Special Różewicz Issue), No. 2, Summer 1991.

——, (Special section on *The Trap*), 5, Spring 1993, pp. 88–111.

Teatr (Special Różewicz Issue), No. 11, 1986.

Henryk Vogler, *Tadeusz Różewicz*, Warsaw, 1972.

——, *Różewicz* (in English), Warsaw, 1976.

Kazimierz Wyka, *Różewicz parokrotnie*, Kraków, 1977.

For Product Safety Concerns and Information please contact our EU representative GPSR@taylorandfrancis.com
Taylor & Francis Verlag GmbH, Kaufingerstraße 24, 80331 München, Germany

www.ingramcontent.com/pod-product-compliance
Lightning Source LLC
Chambersburg PA
CBHW060316240426
43661CB00059B/2781